The Angela Project

FORTY DAYS OF PRAYER
for the Liberation of
American Descendants of Slavery

Cheri L. Mills, Compiler

Edited by Olivia M. Cloud
Cover Design by R. Tyler Anderson

Simmons College of Kentucky
1000 South 4th Street
Louisville, Kentucky 40203
(502) 776-1443
www.simmonscollegeky.edu

ISBN: 978-0-9785572-8-7

SIMMONS
COLLEGE OF KENTUCKY

Please join our prayer community, united in
Forty Days of Prayer for the Liberation of American Descendants of Slavery!

Sign up here!
www.simmonscollegeky.edu

Share your 40 Days of Prayer experience!
#WeAreAngela400SCKY

Table of Contents

"We will have to repent in this generation, not merely for the hateful words and actions of the bad people, but for the appalling silence of the good people. Human progress never rolls in on wheels of inevitability; it comes through the tireless efforts of men willing to be co-workers with God, and without this hard work, time itself becomes an ally of the forces of social stagnation. We must use time creatively, in the knowledge that the time is always ripe to do right."

– Dr. Martin Luther King, Jr.

Introduction

In 1619, forcibly captured Africans arrived in colonial America for the purpose of providing a free labor force to the expanding British territories in the Americas. The year 2019 marks 400 years since the institution of Slavery began with the first "20 and odd Negroes" who were brought to the British colonies. This institution was sustained until the passage of the Thirteenth Amendment. However, as lawyer and social justice activist Bryan Stevenson has observed, "Slavery didn't end in 1865; it just evolved."*

Throughout these 400 years—starting with those enslaved in America and then the American Descendants of Slavery—black people have experienced a Black Holocaust: enslavement, black codes, sharecropping, Jim Crow, lynchings, convict leasing, redlin-ing, restrictive covenants, police brutality, subprime lending, mass incarceration, all of which have resulted in the ghettoization/impoverishment of black communities across America.**

It is at the precipice of this 400th year commemoration that we invite blacks, whites, and people across racial, denominational, and cultural lines to participate in 40 Days of Prayer for the Liberation of American Descendants of Slavery (ADOS). Contained within each daily prayer and reflection page is an excerpt from the documentary, *The Underground Rail Road: A Record*, by William Still. Each excerpt is a direct quote from Mr. Still; therefore, any wording that does not align with standard or contemporary English is reflective of that time.

William Still was an enslaved child, but because of the bravery of his mother, they were able to flee the bondage of slavery. As an adult, William Still committed his life to assisting Black bondservants to freedom through the Underground Rail Road in the 1800s. It is estimated that William assisted over 800 slaves in their quest for freedom. Still's reason for documenting each enslaved's experience was because: "The bondage and deliverance of the children of Israel will never be allowed to sink into oblivion while the world stands. Those scenes of suffering and martyrdom millions of Christians were called upon to pass through in the days of the Inquisition are still subjects of study and have unabated interest for all enlightened minds. The same is true of the history of this country. The struggles of the pioneer fathers are preserved, produced and re-produced, and cherished with undying interest by all Americans, and the day will not arrive while the Republic exists, when these histories will not be found in every library."

Still learned from personal experience that another possible outcome of this documentation was that families could be reunited with loved ones who had fled to freedom. Those fleeing slavery had no roadmaps; they used the North Star as their guide in their quest for freedom.

The second reading on the daily prayer and reflection page is a collection of historical facts revealing the ongoing systemic oppression leveled against our black forebears who were first enslaved and that continued against American Descendants of Slavery.

The third writing on each daily prayer and reflection page is the "We Are the Voice of One" Prayer Declaration, which is adapted from Isaiah 40. We ask that you speak this prayer declaration aloud each day, and then close with your personal prayer.

We encourage you to share this prayer book within your circles of influence — with spiritual partners, church members, organization members, friends, and family members. During these 40 days, you may want to join with others on a teleconference and read the daily reflections together. Be encouraged to join with those of other races or ethnicities. Everyone can pray aloud using the Prayer Declaration, with a designee closing the prayer time and paying homage to those formerly enslaved and their descendants.

*Interview with David Axelrod on *The Axe Files* a podcast from The University of Chicago Institute of Politics and CNN, December 18, 2018.

**Refer to page 99 for a recommended reading list of resources substantiating this statement.

Day 1

Perry's exit was in November, 1853. He was owned by Charles Johnson, who lived at Elkton. The infliction of a severe "flogging" from the hand of his master awakened Perry to consider the importance of the Underground Railroad. Perry had the misfortune to let a "load of fodder upset," about which his master became exasperated, and in his agitated state of mind he succeeded in affixing a number of very ugly stationary marks on Perry's back. However, this was no new thing. Indeed he had suffered at the hands of his mistress even far more keenly than from these "ugly marks." He had but one eye; the other he had been deprived of by a terrible stroke with a cowhide in the "hand of his mistress." This lady he pronounced to be a "perfect savage" and added that "she was in the habit of cowhiding any of her slaves whenever she felt like it, which was quite often." Perry was about twenty-eight years of age and a man of promise.

The Underground Rail Road: A Record
(The True Story of Perry Johnson, of Elkton, Maryland, page 45)

· · · · · · ·

Understanding the Devastation of Slavery

The first 19 or so Africans to reach the English colonies arrived in Jamestown, Virginia, in 1619, brought by Dutch traders who had seized them from a captured Spanish slave ship.

https://en.wikipedia.org/wiki/Slavery_in_the_United_States

Chattel slavery was the American system for the enslavement of Africans. Chattel slavery was structured as involuntary servitude where individuals of African descent became the personal property of another and could be bought, sold or traded. In chattel slavery, enslaved status was passed down to succeeding generations. By contrast, indentured servants were often Europeans who voluntarily sold their labor (or had their labor sold by others) for a certain number of years to pay a debt.

Indentured servitude did not hold lifelong status and was not inherited by children.

"We Are the Voice of One" Prayer Declaration
(Declare Aloud)

We are the Voice of One that crieth in [city and state]: "Prepare Ye the way of the Lord!

Make straight in [city] a highway for our God; Every valley in [city] shall be exalted; And every mountain and hill in [city] shall be brought low. The crooked places in [city] shall be made straight; And the rough places shall be made smooth; And the glory of the Lord shall be revealed in [city and state]; And all of [city] and all nations shall see it together; for the mouth of the Lord has spoken it!"

Heavenly Father, we both claim and proclaim your prophecy that is written in Genesis 15: "Your descendants will be strangers in a foreign land; they will be slaves there and will be treated cruelly for **four hundred years**. But I will punish the nation that enslaves them, and when they leave that foreign land, they will take great wealth with them." Heavenly Father, make us one, just as You and the Lord Jesus are One! Heavenly Father, increase our numbers and gather Your people to pray! Let the Holy Spirit move freely, and the zeal of the Lord of Hosts shall accomplish it! In Jesus' name! Amen!

Offer a Closing Prayer to God
And as you pray....

- Consider the prayers of the enslaved as they lay on the slave ship, stored chained together and stored like cargo for months on an unknown journey that was thousands of miles long. The bodies of the enslaved who died in the Middle Passage were thrown in Atlantic Ocean.

- Imagine the prayers of the enslaved as they fled for freedom, following the North Star despite threats of lynching, beating, mutation, and death.

● Call out the names of the enslaved who were highlighted in today's reading from *The Underground Rail Road* and remember their descendants who still experience systemic racial oppression caused by social engineering.

Day 2

In 1857, this candidate for Canada had the good fortune to escape the clutches of his mistress, Mrs. Elvina Duncans, widow of the late Rev. James Duncans, who lived near Cumberland, Md. He had very serious complaints to allege against his mistress, "who was a member of the Presbyterian Church." To use his own language, "The servants in the house were treated worse than dogs." John was 32 years of age.

The Underground Rail Road: A Record
(The True Story of Samuel Williams,
Alias John Williams, page 82)

· · · · · · ·

U.S. Presidents Who Owned Slaves

George Washington (317): Washington was a major slaveholder before, during, and after his presidency. His will freed his slaves pending the death of his widow, though she freed them within a year of his death.

Thomas Jefferson (600+): Jefferson is believed to have fathered multiple children with his quadroon slave Sally Hemings, the half-sister of late wife Martha Wayles Skelton.

James Madison (100+): Madison proposed the Three-Fifths Compromise, which counted slaves as three fifths of a person for the purposes of taxation and legislative representation. He did not free his slaves in his will.

James Monroe (75): Monroe supported sending freed slaves to the new country of Liberia; its capital, Monrovia, is named after him.

Andrew Jackson (less than 200): Jackson faced several controversies related to slavery during his presidency. During his campaign for office presidency, he faced criticism for being a slave trader. He did not free his slaves in his will.

Martin Van Buren (1): Tom, the only slave Van Buren personally owned, escaped in 1814. When Tom was found in Massachusetts, Van Buren agreed to sell him to the finder, but terms were never finalized and Tom remained free.

William Henry Harrison (11): Harrison inherited several slaves. As the first governor of the Indiana Territory, he unsuccessfully lobbied Congress to legalize slavery there.

John Tyler (70): The tenth U.S. president never freed any of his slaves and consistently supported slavery and its expansion during his time in political office.

James K. Polk (25): Polk became the Democratic nominee for president in 1844, partially because of his tolerance of slavery, and He generally supported slavery as president. His will provided for the freeing of his slaves after the death of his wife, though the Emancipation Proclamation and the Thirteenth Amendment to the Constitution did so long before her death in 1891.

Zachery Taylor (less than 150): Taylor owned slaves throughout his life, but he generally resisted attempts to expand slavery in the territories. After his death, there were rumors that slavery advocates had poisoned him; tests of his body over 100 years later have been inconclusive.

Andrew Johnson (8): Johnson was supportive of Polk's slavery policies. As military governor of Tennessee, he convinced Abraham Lincoln to exempt that area from the Emancipation Proclamation.

Ulysses S. Grant (1): A general in the Union Army, his wife Julia had control of four slaves during the Civil War, given to her by her father. However, it is unclear if she actually was granted legal ownership of them or merely temporary custody. All of them were freed after the Emancipation Proclamation in 1863 (even though the proclamation did not apply to her state of Missouri).

Grant is known to have personally owned one slave, William Jones, from 1857 to 1859.

https://en.wikipedia.org/wiki/List_of_Presidents_of_the_United_States_who_owned_slaves

"We Are the Voice of One" Prayer Declaration
(Declare Aloud)

We are the Voice of One that crieth in [city and state]: "Prepare Ye the way of the Lord!

Make straight in [city] a highway for our God; Every valley in [city] shall be exalted; And every mountain and hill in [city] shall be brought low. The crooked places in [city] shall be made straight; And the rough places shall be made smooth; And the glory of the Lord shall be revealed in [city and state]; And all of [city] and all nations shall see it together; for the mouth of the Lord has spoken it!"

Heavenly Father, we both claim and proclaim your prophecy that is written in Genesis 15: "Your descendants will be strangers in a foreign land; they will be slaves there and will be treated cruelly for **four hundred years**. But I will punish the nation that enslaves them, and when they leave that foreign land, they will take great wealth with them." Heavenly Father, make us one, just as You and the Lord Jesus are One! Heavenly Father, increase our numbers and gather Your people to pray! Let the Holy Spirit move freely, and the zeal of the Lord of Hosts shall accomplish it! In Jesus' name! Amen!

Offer a Closing Prayer to God
And as you pray....

- Consider the prayers of the enslaved as they lay on the slave ship, stored chained together and stored like cargo for months on an unknown journey that was thousands of miles long. The bodies of the enslaved who died in the Middle Passage were thrown in Atlantic Ocean.

- Imagine the prayers of the enslaved as they fled for freedom, following the North Star despite threats of lynching, beating, mutation, and death.

- Call out the names of the enslaved who were highlighted in today's reading from *The Underground Rail Road* and remember their descendants who still experience systemic racial oppression caused by social engineering.

Day 3

About the twenty-ninth of January 1855, Sheridan arrived from the Old Dominion and a life of bondage…Not a great while before making up his mind to escape, for some trifling offence he had been "stretched up with a rope by his hand," and "whipped unmercifully". In addition to this he had "got wind of the fact", that he was to be auctioneered off; …he began to ponder how he could get a ticket on the Underground Railroad and get out of this "place of torment", to where he might have the benefit of his own labor. In this state of mind, about the fourteenth day of November, he took his first and daring step. He went not, however, to learned lawyers or able ministers of the Gospel in his distress and trouble, but wended his way "directly to the woods", where he felt that he would be safer with the wild animals and reptiles, in solitude, than with the barbarous civilization that existed in Portsmouth.

The Underground Rail Road: A Record
(The True Story of Sheridan Ford, page 47)

· · · · · · ·

Treatment of the Enslaved

The power relationships of slavery corrupted many whites who had authority over slaves, with children showing their own cruelty. Masters and overseers resorted to physical punishments to impose their wills. Slaves were punished by whipping, shackling, hanging, beating, burning, mutilation, branding and imprisonment. Punishment was most often meted out in response to disobedience or perceived infractions, but sometimes abuse was carried out to re-assert the dominance of the master or overseer of the slave.

https://en.wikipedia.org/wiki/Slavery_in_the_United_States#Colonial_America

"We Are the Voice of One" Prayer Declaration
(Declare Aloud)

We are the Voice of One that crieth in [city and state]: "Prepare Ye the way of the Lord!

Make straight in [city] a highway for our God; Every valley in [city] shall be exalted; And every mountain and hill in [city] shall be brought low. The crooked places in [city] shall be made straight; And the rough places shall be made smooth; And the glory of the Lord shall be revealed in [city and state]; And all of [city] and all nations shall see it together; for the mouth of the Lord has spoken it!"

Heavenly Father, we both claim and proclaim your prophecy that is written in Genesis 15: "Your descendants will be strangers in a foreign land; they will be slaves there and will be treated cruelly for **four hundred years**. But I will punish the nation that enslaves them, and when they leave that foreign land, they will take great wealth with them." Heavenly Father, make us one, just as You and the Lord Jesus are One! Heavenly Father, increase our numbers and gather Your people to pray! Let the Holy Spirit move freely, and the zeal of the Lord of Hosts shall accomplish it! In Jesus' name! Amen!

Offer a Closing Prayer to God
And as you pray....

- Consider the prayers of the enslaved as they lay on the slave ship, stored chained together and stored like cargo for months on an unknown journey that was thousands of miles long. The bodies of the enslaved who died in the Middle Passage were thrown in Atlantic Ocean.

- Imagine the prayers of the enslaved as they fled for freedom, following the North Star despite threats of lynching, beating, mutation, and death.

- Call out the names of the enslaved who were highlighted in today's reading from *The Underground Rail Road* and remember their descendants who still experience systemic racial oppression caused by social engineering.

Day 4

June 4, 1857 — Edward is a hardy and firm-looking young man of twenty-four years of age, chestnut color, medium size, and "likely", - would doubtless bring $1,400 in the market. He had been held as the property of the widow, "Betsy Brown", who resided near Mill Green P.O., in Hartford county, Md. "She was a very bad woman; would go to church every Sunday, come home and go to fighting amongst the colored people; was never satisfied; she treated my mother very hard, (said Ed.): would beat her with a walking stick. She was an old woman and belonged to the Catholic Church. Over her slaves she kept an overseer, who was a very wicked man; very bad on colored people; his name was "Bill Eddy"; Elizabeth Brown owned twelve head."

The Underground Rail Road: A Record
(The True Story of Edward Morgan, page 50)

· · · · · · ·

Treatment of the Enslaved

William Wells Brown, who escaped to freedom, reported that on one plantation, slave men were required to pick eighty pounds per day of cotton, while women were required to pick seventy pounds; if any slave failed in his or her quota, they were subject to whip lashes for each pound they were short. The whipping post stood next to the cotton scales. A New York man who attended a slave auction in the mid-19th Century reported that at least three-quarters of the male slaves he saw at sale had scars on their backs from whipping.

https://en.wikipedia.org/wiki/Slavery_in_the_United_States#Colonial_America

"We are the Voice of One" Prayer Declaration
(Declare Aloud)

We are the Voice of One that crieth in [city and state]: "Prepare Ye the way of the Lord!

Make straight in [city] a highway for our God; Every valley in [city] shall be exalted; And every mountain and hill in [city] shall be brought low. The crooked places in [city] shall be made straight; And the rough places shall be made smooth; And the glory of the Lord shall be revealed in [city and state]; And all of [city] and all nations shall see it together; for the mouth of the Lord has spoken it!"

Heavenly Father, we both claim and proclaim your prophecy that is written in Genesis 15: "Your descendants will be strangers in a foreign land; they will be slaves there and will be treated cruelly for **four hundred years**. But I will punish the nation that enslaves them, and when they leave that foreign land, they will take great wealth with them." Heavenly Father, make us one, just as You and the Lord Jesus are One! Heavenly Father, increase our numbers and gather Your people to pray! Let the Holy Spirit move freely, and the zeal of the Lord of Hosts shall accomplish it! In Jesus' name! Amen!

Offer a Closing Prayer to God
And as you pray....

- Consider the prayers of the enslaved as they lay on the slave ship, stored chained together and stored like cargo for months on an unknown journey that was thousands of miles long. The bodies of the enslaved who died in the Middle Passage were thrown in Atlantic Ocean.

- Imagine the prayers of the enslaved as they fled for freedom, following the North Star despite threats of lynching, beating, mutation, and death.

- Call out the names of the enslaved who were highlighted in today's reading from *The Underground Rail Road* and remember their descendants who still experience systemic racial oppression caused by social engineering.

Day 5

June 4, 1857 — "James is about twenty-one years of age, full black, and medium size. As he had been worked hard on poor fare, he concluded to leave, in company with his brother and two cousins, leaving his parents in slavery, owned by the "Widow Pyle," who was also the owner of himself. "She was upwards of eighty, very passionate and ill-natured, although a member of the Presbyterian Church." James may be worth $1,400."

The Underground Rail Road: A Record
(The True Story of James Butler, page 50)

· · · · · · ·

"Found Voices," from ABC News' *Nightline* (aired January 12, 1999), featuring the actual voices of former slaves taken from interviews conducted in 1930s and 40s:

"They sold us like we were horses and cows. They put you up on a bench and bid on you like you were cattle."

"Colored people didn't have no beds, they just slept on the floor like wild people. We didn't know nothing. They wouldn't allow you to look at a book."

Fountain Hughes

·

"I can remember it like it was yesterday. They took that poor ol' woman, carried her in the peach orchard and whipped her. And, you know, just tied her hand this a way, you know, 'round the peach orchard tree. They had her clothes off down to her waist. And every now and then they'd whip her, you know, and then snuff the pipe out on her. You know the embers in the pipe." (They'd blow the embers on her.)

"Momma and them didn't know where to go after freedom broke. They just turned you out like you turn out cattle."

Laura Smalley

"We Are the Voice of One" Prayer Declaration
(Declare Aloud)

We are the Voice of One that crieth in [city and state]: "Prepare Ye the way of the Lord!

Make straight in [city] a highway for our God; Every valley in [city] shall be exalted; And every mountain and hill in [city] shall be brought low. The crooked places in [city] shall be made straight; And the rough places shall be made smooth; And the glory of the Lord shall be revealed in [city and state]; And all of [city] and all nations shall see it together; for the mouth of the Lord has spoken it!"

Heavenly Father, we both claim and proclaim your prophecy that is written in Genesis 15: "Your descendants will be strangers in a foreign land; they will be slaves there and will be treated cruelly for **four hundred years**. But I will punish the nation that enslaves them, and when they leave that foreign land, they will take great wealth with them." Heavenly Father, make us one, just as You and the Lord Jesus are One! Heavenly Father, increase our numbers and gather Your people to pray! Let the Holy Spirit move freely, and the zeal of the Lord of Hosts shall accomplish it! In Jesus' name! Amen!

Offer a Closing Prayer to God
And as you pray....

- Consider the prayers of the enslaved as they lay on the slave ship, stored chained together and stored like cargo for months on an

unknown journey that was thousands of miles long. The bodies of the enslaved who died in the Middle Passage were thrown in Atlantic Ocean.

- Imagine the prayers of the enslaved as they fled for freedom, following the North Star despite threats of lynching, beating, mutation, and death.

- Call out the names of the enslaved who were highlighted in today's reading from *The Underground Rail Road* and remember their descendants who still experience systemic racial oppression caused by social engineering.

Day 6

About the 1st of March, 1855, Mary was presented to the Vigilance Committee. She was of agreeable manners, about forty-five years of age, dark complexion, round built, and intelligent. She had been the mother of fifteen children, four of whom had been sold away from her; one was still held in slavery in Petersburg; the others were all dead. At the sale of one of her children she was so affected with grief that she was thrown into violent convulsions, which caused the loss of her speech for one entire month. But this little episode was not a matter to excite sympathy in the breasts of the highly refined and tender-hearted Christian mothers of Petersburg.

The Underground Rail Road: A Record
(The True Story of Mary Epps, Alias Emma Brown, pages 52-53)

· · · · · · ·

Convict Leasing

With Emancipation a legal reality, white Southerners were concerned with both controlling the newly freed slaves and keeping them in the labor force at the lowest level. The system of convict leasing began during Reconstruction and was fully implemented in the 1880s. The practice officially ended in the last state, Alabama, in 1928. Convict leasing persisted in various forms until it was abolished in 1942 by President Franklin D. Roosevelt during World War II, several months after the attack on Pearl Harbor involved the U.S. in the conflict. This system allowed private contractors to purchase the services of convicts from state or local governments for a specific time period. African Americans, due to "vigorous and selective enforcement of laws and discriminatory sentencing," made up the vast majority of the convicts leased.

https://en.wikipedia.org/wiki/Slavery_in_the_United_States#Colonial_America

"We Are the Voice of One" Prayer Declaration
(Declare Aloud)

We are the Voice of One that crieth in [city and state]: "Prepare Ye the way of the Lord!

Make straight in [city] a highway for our God; Every valley in [city] shall be exalted; And every mountain and hill in [city] shall be brought low. The crooked places in [city] shall be made straight; And the rough places shall be made smooth; And the glory of the Lord shall be revealed in [city and state]; And all of [city] and all nations shall see it together; for the mouth of the Lord has spoken it!"

Heavenly Father, we both claim and proclaim your prophecy that is written in Genesis 15: "Your descendants will be strangers in a foreign land; they will be slaves there and will be treated cruelly for **four hundred years**. But I will punish the nation that enslaves them, and when they leave that foreign land, they will take great wealth with them." Heavenly Father, make us one, just as You and the Lord Jesus are One! Heavenly Father, increase our numbers and gather Your people to pray! Let the Holy Spirit move freely, and the zeal of the Lord of Hosts shall accomplish it! In Jesus' name! Amen!

Offer a Closing Prayer to God
And as you pray....

- Consider the prayers of the enslaved as they lay on the slave ship, stored chained together and stored like cargo for months on an unknown journey that was thousands of miles long. The bodies of the enslaved who died in the Middle Passage were thrown in Atlantic Ocean.

- Imagine the prayers of the enslaved as they fled for freedom, following the North Star despite threats of lynching, beating, mutation, and death.

- Call out the names of the enslaved who were highlighted in today's reading from *The Underground Rail Road* and remember their descendants who still experience systemic racial oppression caused by social engineering.

Day 7

The wife of his bosom and his four children, only five days before he fled, were sold to a trader in Richmond, VA for no other offence than simply 'because she had resisted' the lustful designs of her master, being 'true to her own companion.' After this poor slave mother and her children were cast into prison for sale, the husband and some of his friends tried hard to find a purchaser in the neighborhood; but the malicious and brutal master refused to sell her — wishing to gratify his malice to the utmost, and to punish his victims all that lay in his power....

The Underground Rail Road: A Record
(The True Story of Robert Brown,
Alias Thomas Jones, pages 80-81)

. . . .

Black Codes

The Black Codes were laws passed by Southern states in 1865 and 1866 after the American Civil War with the intent and the effect of restricting African Americans' freedom, and of compelling them to work in a labor economy based on low wages or debt. Black Codes were part of a larger pattern of Southern whites, who were trying to suppress the new freedom of formerly enslaved African Americans, the freedmen. Black codes were essentially replacements for slave codes in those states. Before the war, Black Codes were enacted in states that prohibited slavery. Ohio, Illinois, Indiana, Michigan, and New York enacted Black Codes to discourage free blacks from residing in those states and to deny them equal rights, including the right to vote, the right to public education, and the right to equal treatment under the law. Some of these northern Black Codes were repealed around the same time that the Civil War ended and slavery was abolished.

https://en.wikipedia.org/wiki/Black_Codes_(United_States)

"We Are the Voice of One" Prayer Declaration
(Declare Aloud)

We are the Voice of One that crieth in [city and state]: "Prepare Ye the way of the Lord!

Make straight in [city] a highway for our God; Every valley in [city] shall be exalted; And every mountain and hill in [city] shall be brought low. The crooked places in [city] shall be made straight; And the rough places shall be made smooth; And the glory of the Lord shall be revealed in [city and state]; And all of [city] and all nations shall see it together; for the mouth of the Lord has spoken it!"

Heavenly Father, we both claim and proclaim your prophecy that is written in Genesis 15: "Your descendants will be strangers in a foreign land; they will be slaves there and will be treated cruelly for **four hundred years**. But I will punish the nation that enslaves them, and when they leave that foreign land, they will take great wealth with them." Heavenly Father, make us one, just as You and the Lord Jesus are One! Heavenly Father, increase our numbers and gather Your people to pray! Let the Holy Spirit move freely, and the zeal of the Lord of Hosts shall accomplish it! In Jesus' name! Amen!

Offer a Closing Prayer to God
And as you pray....

- Consider the prayers of the enslaved as they lay on the slave ship, stored chained together and stored like cargo for months on an unknown journey that was thousands of miles long. The bodies of the enslaved who died in the Middle Passage were thrown in Atlantic Ocean.

- Imagine the prayers of the enslaved as they fled for freedom, following the North Star despite threats of lynching, beating, mutation, and death.

- Call out the names of the enslaved who were highlighted in today's reading from *The Underground Rail Road* and remember their descendants who still experience systemic racial oppression caused by social engineering.

Day 8

Alfred is twenty-three years of age, in statue quite small, full black, and bears the marks of ill usage. Though a member of the Methodist Church, his master, Fletcher Jackson, 'thought nothing of taking the shovel to Alfred's head; or of knocking him, and stamping his head with the heels of his boots.' Repeatedly, of late, he had been shockingly beaten. To escape those terrible visitations, therefore, he made up his mind to seek a refuge in Canada.

The Underground Rail Road: A Record
(The True Story of Alfred Goulden, page 90)

. . . .

Black Codes

Since the colonial period, colonies and states had passed laws that discriminated against free blacks. In the South, these were generally included in "slave codes," the goal being to reduce the influence potential of free blacks on the enslaved (particularly after slave rebellions). Restrictions included prohibiting free blacks from voting (although North Carolina allowed this before 1831), bearing arms, gathering in groups for worship, and learning to read and write. A major purpose of these laws was to preserve slavery.

In the first two years after the Civil War, white-dominated southern legislatures passed Black Codes modeled after the earlier slave codes. They were particularly concerned with controlling movement and labor, as Slavery had given way to a free labor system. Although freedmen had been emancipated, their lives were greatly restricted by the Black Codes.

https://en.wikipedia.org/wiki/Black_Codes_(United_States)

"We Are the Voice of One" Prayer Declaration
(Declare Aloud)

We are the Voice of One that crieth in [city and state]: "Prepare Ye the way of the Lord!

Make straight in [city] a highway for our God; Every valley in [city] shall be exalted; And every mountain and hill in [city] shall be brought low. The crooked places in [city] shall be made straight; And the rough places shall be made smooth; And the glory of the Lord shall be revealed in [city and state]; And all of [city] and all nations shall see it together; for the mouth of the Lord has spoken it!"

Heavenly Father, we both claim and proclaim your prophecy that is written in Genesis 15: "Your descendants will be strangers in a foreign land; they will be slaves there and will be treated cruelly for **four hundred years**. But I will punish the nation that enslaves them, and when they leave that foreign land, they will take great wealth with them." Heavenly Father, make us one, just as You and the Lord Jesus are One! Heavenly Father, increase our numbers and gather Your people to pray! Let the Holy Spirit move freely, and the zeal of the Lord of Hosts shall accomplish it! In Jesus' name! Amen!

Offer a Closing Prayer to God
And as you pray....

- Consider the prayers of the enslaved as they lay on the slave ship, stored chained together and stored like cargo for months on an unknown journey that was thousands of miles long. The bodies of the enslaved who died in the Middle Passage were thrown in Atlantic Ocean.

- Imagine the prayers of the enslaved as they fled for freedom, following the North Star despite threats of lynching, beating, mutation, and death.

- Call out the names of the enslaved who were highlighted in today's reading from *The Underground Rail Road* and remember their descendants who still experience systemic racial oppression caused by social engineering.

Day 9

Perry was about thirty-one years of age, round-made, of dark complexion, and looked quite gratified with his expedition, and the prospect of becoming a British subject instead of a Maryland slave. He was not free, however, from the sad thoughts of having left his wife and three children in the 'prison house,' nor of the fact that his own dear mother was brutally stabbed to the heart with a butcher knife by her young master, while he [Perry] was a babe....

The Underground Rail Road: A Record
(The True Story of Perry Henry Trusty, page 95)

. . . .

Erosion of the 13th, 14th and 15th Amendments

The Thirteenth Amendment (proposed in 1864 and ratified in 1865) abolished Slavery and involuntary servitude, except for those duly convicted of a crime. The Fourteenth Amendment (proposed in 1866 and ratified in 1868) addresses citizenship rights and equal protection of the laws for all persons. The Fifteenth Amendment (proposed in 1869 and ratified in 1870) prohibits discrimination in voting rights of citizens on the basis of "race, color, or previous condition of servitude." All races, regardless of prior slavery, could vote in some states of the early United States, such as New Jersey, provided that they could meet other requirements, such as property ownership.

These amendments were intended to guarantee freedom to the formerly enslaved and to establish and prevent discrimination in certain civil rights to the formerly enslaved and to all citizens of the United States. The promise of these amendments was eroded by state laws and federal court decisions over the course of the 19th Century. In 1876 and later, some states passed Jim Crow laws that limited the rights of African Americans. Important Supreme Court decisions that undermined these amendments were the Slaughter-House cases in 1873, which prevented rights guaranteed under the Fourteenth Amendment's privileges or immunities clause from being extended to rights under state law; and *Plessy v. Ferguson* in 1896, which originated the phrase "separate but equal" and gave federal approval to Jim Crow laws.

https://en.wikipedia.org/wiki/Reconstruction_Amendments

"We Are the Voice of One" Prayer Declaration
(Declare Aloud)

We are the Voice of One that crieth in [city and state]: "Prepare Ye the way of the Lord!

Make straight in [city] a highway for our God; Every valley in [city] shall be exalted; And every mountain and hill in [city] shall be brought low. The crooked places in [city] shall be made straight; And the rough places shall be made smooth; And the glory of the Lord shall be revealed in [city and state]; And all of [city] and all nations shall see it together; for the mouth of the Lord has spoken it!"

Heavenly Father, we both claim and proclaim your prophecy that is written in Genesis 15: "Your descendants will be strangers in a foreign land; they will be slaves there and will be treated cruelly for **four**

hundred years. But I will punish the nation that enslaves them, and when they leave that foreign land, they will take great wealth with them." Heavenly Father, make us one, just as You and the Lord Jesus are One! Heavenly Father, increase our numbers and gather Your people to pray! Let the Holy Spirit move freely, and the zeal of the Lord of Hosts shall accomplish it! In Jesus' name! Amen!

Offer a Closing Prayer to God
And as you pray....

- Consider the prayers of the enslaved as they lay on the slave ship, stored chained together and stored like cargo for months on an unknown journey that was thousands of miles long. The bodies of the enslaved who died in the Middle Passage were thrown in Atlantic Ocean.

- Imagine the prayers of the enslaved as they fled for freedom, following the North Star despite threats of lynching, beating, mutation, and death.

- Call out the names of the enslaved who were highlighted in today's reading from *The Underground Rail Road* and remember their descendants who still experience systemic racial oppression caused by social engineering.

Day 10 _____

Emanuel was about twenty-five years of age, with seven-eighths of white blood in his veins, medium size, and a very smart and likely-looking piece of property generally. He had the good fortune to escape from Edward H. Hubbert, a ship timber merchant of Norfolk, Va. Under Hubbert's yoke he had served only five years, having been bought by him from a certain Aldridge Mandrey, who was described as a 'very cruel man,' and would 'rather fight than eat.' 'I have licks that will carry me to my grave, and will be there till the flesh rots off my bones,' said Emanuel, adding that his master was a 'devil,' though a member of the Reformed Methodist Church.

The Underground Rail Road: A Record
(The True Story of Emanuel T. White, page 101)

• • • • • • •

Jim Crow Laws

Jim Crow laws were state and local laws that enforced racial segregation in the Southern United States. All were enacted in the late 19th and early 20th centuries by white Democratic-dominated state legislatures after the Reconstruction period. The laws were enforced in some form until 1965. In practice, Jim Crow laws mandated racial segregation in all public facilities in the states of the former Confederate States of America, starting in the 1870s and 1880s, and were upheld in 1896, by the U.S. Supreme Court's "separate but equal" legal doctrine for facilities for African Americans, established with the court's decision in the case of *Plessy vs. Ferguson*. Moreover, public education had essentially been segregated since its establishment in most of the South, after the Civil War (1861–65).

The legal principle of "separate, but equal" racial segregation was extended to public facilities and transportation, including the coaches of interstate trains and buses. Facilities for African Americans…were consistently inferior and underfunded, compared to the facilities for white Americans

https://en.wikipedia.org/wiki/Jim_Crow_laws

"We Are the Voice of One" Prayer Declaration
(Declare Aloud)

We are the Voice of One that crieth in [city and state]: "Prepare Ye the way of the Lord!

Make straight in [city] a highway for our God; Every valley in [city] shall be exalted; And every mountain and hill in [city] shall be brought low. The crooked places in [city] shall be made straight; And the rough places shall be made smooth; And the glory of the Lord shall be revealed in [city and state]; And all of [city] and all nations shall see it together; for the mouth of the Lord has spoken it!"

Heavenly Father, we both claim and proclaim your prophecy that is written in Genesis 15: "Your descendants will be strangers in a foreign land; they will be slaves there and will be treated cruelly for **four hundred years**. But I will punish the nation that enslaves them, and when they leave that foreign land, they will take great wealth with them." Heavenly Father, make us one, just as You and the Lord Jesus are One! Heavenly Father, increase our numbers and gather Your people to pray! Let the Holy Spirit move freely, and the zeal of the Lord of Hosts shall accomplish it! In Jesus' name! Amen!

Offer a Closing Prayer to God
And as you pray....

- Consider the prayers of the enslaved as they lay on the slave ship, stored chained together and stored like cargo for months on an unknown journey that was thousands of miles long. The bodies of the enslaved who died in the Middle Passage were thrown in Atlantic Ocean.

- Imagine the prayers of the enslaved as they fled for freedom, following the North Star despite threats of lynching, beating, mutation, and death.

- Call out the names of the enslaved who were highlighted in today's reading from *The Underground Rail Road* and remember their descendants who still experience systemic racial oppression caused by social engineering.

Day 11

His master unceremoniously, without intimating in any way to John, that he was to be sold, took him to Richmond, on the first day of January (the great annual sale day), and directly to the slave-auction. Just as John was being taken into the building, was invited to submit to hand-cuffs. As the thought flashed upon his mind that he was about to be sold on the auction-block, he grew terribly desperate. 'Liberty or death' was the watchword of that awful moment. In the twinkling of an eye, he turned on his enemies, with his fist, knife, and feet, so tiger-like, that he actually put four or five men to flight, his master among the number. His enemies thus suddenly baffled, John wheeled, and, as if assisted by an angel, strange as it may appear, was soon out of sight of his pursuers, and securely hid away. This was the last hour of John Henry's slave life, but not, however, of his struggles and sufferings for freedom, for before a final chance to escape presented itself, nine months elapsed.

The Underground Rail Road: A Record
(The True Story of John Henry, pages 126-127)

· · · · · · ·

The New York City Draft Riots

The New York City draft riots (July 13–16, 1863), known at the time as Draft Week, were violent disturbances in Lower Manhattan, widely regarded as the culmination of white working-class discontent with new laws passed by Congress to draft men to fight in the ongoing American Civil War. The riots remain the largest civil and racially-charged insurrection in American history, aside from the Civil War itself....

Initially intended to express anger at the draft, the protests turned into a race riot, with white rioters, predominantly Irish immigrants, attacking black people throughout the city. The official death toll was listed at about 120 individuals. Conditions in the city were such that Major General John E. Wool, commander of the Department of the East, said on July 16 that,

"Martial law ought to be proclaimed, but I have not a sufficient force to enforce it."

The military did not reach the city until the second day of rioting, by which time the mobs had ransacked or destroyed numerous public buildings, two Protestant churches, the homes of various abolitionists or sympathizers, many black homes, and the Colored Orphan Asylum at 44th Street and Fifth Avenue, which was burned to the ground. The area's demographics changed as a result of the riot. Many black residents left Manhattan permanently, with many moving to Brooklyn. By 1865, the black population fell below 11,000 for the first time since 1820.

https://en.wikipedia.org/wiki/New_York_City_draft_riots

"We Are the Voice of One" Prayer Declaration
(Declare Aloud)

We are the Voice of One that crieth in [city and state]: "Prepare Ye the way of the Lord!

Make straight in [city] a highway for our God; Every valley in [city] shall be exalted; And every mountain and hill in [city] shall be brought low. The crooked places in [city] shall be made straight; And the rough places shall be made smooth; And the glory of the Lord shall be revealed in [city and state]; And all of [city] and all nations shall see it together; for the mouth of the Lord has spoken it!"

Heavenly Father, we both claim and proclaim your prophecy that is written in Genesis 15: "Your descendants will be strangers in a foreign land; they will be slaves there and will be treated cruelly for **four hundred years**. But I will punish the nation that enslaves them, and when they leave that foreign land, they will take great wealth with them." Heavenly Father, make us one, just as You and the Lord Jesus are One! Heavenly Father, increase our numbers and gather Your people to pray! Let the Holy Spirit move freely, and the zeal of the Lord of Hosts shall accomplish it! In Jesus' name! Amen!

Offer a Closing Prayer to God
And as you pray....

- Consider the prayers of the enslaved as they lay on the slave ship, stored chained together and stored like cargo for months on an unknown journey that was thousands of miles long. The bodies of the enslaved who died in the Middle Passage were thrown in Atlantic Ocean.

- Imagine the prayers of the enslaved as they fled for freedom, following the North Star despite threats of lynching, beating, mutation, and death.

- Call out the names of the enslaved who were highlighted in today's reading from *The Underground Rail Road* and remember their descendants who still experience systemic racial oppression caused by social engineering.

Day 12

For a number of years Hezekiah had been laboring under the pleasing thought that he should succeed in obtaining freedom through purchase, having had an understanding with his owner with this object in view. At different times he had paid on account for himself nineteen hundred dollars, six hundred dollars more than he was to have paid according to the first agreement. Although so shamefully defrauded in the first instance, he concluded to bear the disappointment as patiently as possible and get out of the lion's mouth as best he could. He continued to work on and save his money until he had actually come within one hundred dollars of paying two thousand. At this point instead of getting his free papers, as he firmly believed that he should, to his surprise one day he saw a notorious trader approaching the shop where he was at work. The errand of the trader was soon made known. Hezekiah simply requested time to go back to the other end of the shop to get his coat, which he seized and ran... he had left his wife Louisa, and two little boys, Henry and Manuel.

The Underground Rail Road: A Record
(The True Story of Hezekiah Hill, page 135)

· · · · · · ·

Lynchings

Most lynchings were of African-American men in the South, but women also were lynched. White lynchings of blacks also occurred in Midwestern and border states, especially during the 20th-century Great Migration of blacks out of the South. The purpose was to enforce white supremacy and intimidate blacks through racial terrorism.

Some hangings were professionally photographed and sold as postcards, which were popular souvenirs in some parts of the U.S. Victims were killed by mobs in a variety of other ways: shot repeatedly, burned alive, forced to jump off a bridge, dragged behind cars. Sometimes they were tortured as well, with body parts sometimes removed and sold as souvenirs.

Michael J. Pfeifer, professor of history at John Jay College of Criminal Justice and the CUNY Graduate Center cites "the modern, racialized excesses of urban police forces in the twentieth century and after" as having characteristics of lynching. "More black people [were] killed by cops in 2015 than were lynched in the worst year of Jim Crow."

https://en.wikipedia.org/wiki/Lynching_in_the_United_States

"We Are the Voice of One" Prayer Declaration
(Declare Aloud)

We are the Voice of One that crieth in [city and state]: "Prepare Ye the way of the Lord!

Make straight in [city] a highway for our God; Every valley in [city] shall be exalted; And every mountain and hill in [city] shall be brought low. The crooked places in [city] shall be made straight; And the rough places shall be made smooth; And the glory of the Lord shall be revealed in [city and state]; And all of [city] and all nations shall see it together; for the mouth of the Lord has spoken it!"

Heavenly Father, we both claim and proclaim your prophecy that is written in Genesis 15: "Your descendants will be strangers in a foreign land; they will be slaves there and will be treated cruelly for **four hundred years**. But I will punish the nation that enslaves them, and when they leave that foreign land, they will take great wealth with them." Heavenly Father, make us one, just as You and the Lord Jesus are One! Heavenly Father, increase our numbers and gather Your people to pray! Let the Holy Spirit move freely, and the zeal of the Lord of Hosts shall accomplish it! In Jesus' name! Amen!

Offer a Closing Prayer to God
And as you pray....

- Consider the prayers of the enslaved as they lay on the slave ship, stored chained together and stored like cargo for months on an unknown journey that was thousands of miles long. The bodies of the enslaved who died in the Middle Passage were thrown in Atlantic Ocean.
- Imagine the prayers of the enslaved as they fled for freedom, following the North Star despite threats of lynching, beating, mutation, and death.
- Call out the names of the enslaved who were highlighted in today's reading from *The Underground Rail Road* and remember their descendants who still experience systemic racial oppression caused by social engineering.

Day 13

Robert was about thirty years of age, dark color, quite tall, and in talking with him a little while, it was soon discovered that Slavery had not crushed all the brains out of his head by a good deal... According to law he was entitled to his freedom at the age of twenty-five. But what right had a negro, which white slave-holders were 'bound to respect?' Many who had been willed free, were held just as firmly in Slavery, as if no will had ever been made. Robert had too much sense to suppose that he could gain anything by seeking legal redress. This method, therefore, was considered out of the question. But in the meantime he was growing very naturally in favor of the Underground Rail Road. From his experience Robert did not hesitate to say that his master was 'mean', a 'very hard man', who would work his servants early and late, without allowing them food and clothing sufficient to shield them from the cold and hunger. Robert certainly had unmistakable marks about him, of having been used roughly.

The Underground Rail Road: A Record
(The True Story of Robert Fisher, page 138)

· · · · · · · ·

Slave Patrols

Slave patrols were organized groups of predominantly white men who monitored and enforced discipline upon black slaves in the antebellum U.S. southern states. The slave patrols' function was to police slaves, especially runaways and defiant slaves. They also formed river patrols to prevent escape by boat. Slave patrols were first established in South Carolina in 1704, and the idea spread throughout the colonies.

https://en.wikipedia.org/wiki/Slave_patrol

"We Are the Voice of One" Prayer Declaration
(Declare Aloud)

We are the Voice of One that crieth in [city and state]: "Prepare Ye the way of the Lord!

Make straight in [city] a highway for our God; Every valley in [city] shall be exalted; And every mountain and hill in [city] shall be brought low. The crooked places in [city] shall be made straight; And the rough places shall be made smooth; And the glory of the Lord shall be revealed in [city and state]; And all of [city] and all nations shall see it together; for the mouth of the Lord has spoken it!"

Heavenly Father, we both claim and proclaim your prophecy that is written in Genesis 15: "Your descendants will be strangers in a foreign land; they will be slaves there and will be treated cruelly for **four hundred years**. But I will punish the nation that enslaves them, and when they leave that foreign land, they will take great wealth with them." Heavenly Father, make us one, just as You and the Lord Jesus are One! Heavenly Father, increase our numbers and gather Your people to pray! Let the Holy Spirit move freely, and the zeal of the Lord of Hosts shall accomplish it! In Jesus' name! Amen!

Offer a Closing Prayer to God
And as you pray....

- Consider the prayers of the enslaved as they lay on the slave ship, stored chained together and stored like cargo for months on an unknown journey that was thousands of miles long. The bodies of the enslaved who died in the Middle Passage were thrown in Atlantic Ocean.

- Imagine the prayers of the enslaved as they fled for freedom, following the North Star despite threats of lynching, beating, mutation, and death.

- Call out the names of the enslaved who were highlighted in today's reading from *The Underground Rail Road* and remember their descendants who still experience systemic racial oppression caused by social engineering.

Day 14

"Mary arrived with her two children in the early Spring of 1854. The mother was a woman of about thirty-three years of age, quite tall, with a countenance and general appearance well fitted to awaken sympathy at first sight. Her oldest child was a little girl seven years of age, named Lydia; the other was named Louisa Caroline, three years of age, both promising in appearance. They were the so called property of John Ennis, of Georgetown, Delaware. For their flight they chose the dead of Winter…Until she was convinced that her two children were to be sold, she could not quite muster courage to set out on the journey…To bind up the broken heart of such a poor slave mother, and to aid such tender plants as were these little girls, from such a wretched state of barbarism as existed in poor little Delaware, was doubly gratifying to the Committee."

The Underground Rail Road: A Record
(The True Story of Mary Ennis alias Licia Hemmin, page 139)

· · · · · · ·

Slave Patrols

Slaves who were encountered without passes were expected to be returned to their owners, as stated in the slave code. Punishment for runaway slaves could be expected. Black persons were subjected to questioning, searches, and other forms of harassment. Oftentimes, whippings and beatings for non-compliant, and even compliant slaves, could be expected. More than floggings and beatings, however, slaves feared the threat of being placed on the auction block and being separated from their families. If caught by patrols and returned to their masters, being placed on the auction block was an option for masters who no longer wanted to deal with their non-compliant slaves. During these times, slaves were often neglected and mistreated despite having permission to travel.

https://en.wikipedia.org/wiki/Slave_patrol

"We Are the Voice of One" Prayer Declaration
(Declare Aloud)

We are the Voice of One that crieth in [city and state]: "Prepare Ye the way of the Lord!

Make straight in [city] a highway for our God; Every valley in [city] shall be exalted; And every mountain and hill in [city] shall be brought low. The crooked places in [city] shall be made straight; And the rough places shall be made smooth; And the glory of the Lord shall be revealed in [city and state]; And all of [city] and all nations shall see it together; for the mouth of the Lord has spoken it!"

Heavenly Father, we both claim and proclaim your prophecy that is written in Genesis 15: "Your descendants will be strangers in a foreign land; they will be slaves there and will be treated cruelly for **four hundred years**. But I will punish the nation that enslaves them, and when they leave that foreign land, they will take great wealth with them." Heavenly Father, make us one, just as You and the Lord Jesus are One! Heavenly Father, increase our numbers and gather Your people to pray! Let the Holy Spirit move freely, and the zeal of the Lord of Hosts shall accomplish it! In Jesus' name! Amen!

Offer a Closing Prayer to God
And as you pray....

- Consider the prayers of the enslaved as they lay on the slave ship, stored chained together and stored like cargo for months on an unknown journey that was thousands of miles long. The bodies of the enslaved who died in the Middle Passage were thrown in Atlantic Ocean.

- Imagine the prayers of the enslaved as they fled for freedom, following the North Star despite threats of lynching, beating, mutation, and death.

- Call out the names of the enslaved who were highlighted in today's reading from *The Underground Rail Road* and remember their descendants who still experience systemic racial oppression caused by social engineering.

Day 15 ⎯⎯⎯⎯⎯⎯⎯⎯⎯⎯⎯⎯⎯⎯⎯

"Susan was also a passenger on the same ship that brought Wm. B. White. She was from Norfolk. Her toil, body and strength were claimed by Thomas Eckels, Esq., a man of wealth and likewise a man of intemperance...for four months, like a true and earnest woman, she endured a great "fight of affliction," in this horrible place. But the thought of freedom enabled her to keep her courage up, until the glad news was conveyed to her that all things were ready, providing that she could get safely to the boat, on which she was to be secreted...She left one sister, named Mary Ann Tharagood, who was wanting to come away very much. Susan was a woman of dark color, round built, medium height, and about forty years of age when she escaped in 1854."

The Underground Rail Road: A Record
(The True Story of Susan Brooks, page 142)

. . . .

State Militias as Patrollers

State militia groups were also organized from among the cadets of the Southern military academies, of The Citadel and the Virginia Military Institute, which were founded to provide a military command structure and discipline within the slave patrols and to detect, encounter, and crush any organized slave meetings that might lead to revolt or rebellion.

https://en.wikipedia.org/wiki/Slave_patrol

"We Are the Voice of One" Prayer Declaration
(Declare Aloud)

We are the Voice of One that crieth in [city and state]: "Prepare Ye the way of the Lord!

Make straight in [city] a highway for our God; Every valley in [city] shall be exalted; And every mountain and hill in [city] shall be brought low. The crooked places in [city] shall be made straight; And the rough places shall be made smooth; And the glory of the Lord shall be revealed in [city and state]; And all of [city] and all nations shall see it together; for the mouth of the Lord has spoken it!"

Heavenly Father, we both claim and proclaim your prophecy that is written in Genesis 15: "Your descendants will be strangers in a foreign land; they will be slaves there and will be treated cruelly for **four hundred years**. But I will punish the nation that enslaves them, and when they leave that foreign land, they will take great wealth with them." Heavenly Father, make us one, just as You and the Lord Jesus are One! Heavenly Father, increase our numbers and gather Your people to pray! Let the Holy Spirit move freely, and the zeal of the Lord of Hosts shall accomplish it! In Jesus' name! Amen!

Offer a Closing Prayer to God
And as you pray....

- Consider the prayers of the enslaved as they lay on the slave ship, stored chained together and stored like cargo for months on an unknown journey that was thousands of miles long. The bodies of the enslaved who died in the Middle Passage were thrown in Atlantic Ocean.

- Imagine the prayers of the enslaved as they fled for freedom, following the North Star despite threats of lynching, beating, mutation, and death.

- Call out the names of the enslaved who were highlighted in today's reading from *The Underground Rail Road* and remember their descendants who still experience systemic racial oppression caused by social engineering.

Day 16 _____

"James was about thirty-two years of age, medium size, and of an agreeable appearance. He was owned by a maiden lady, who lived at Williamsburg...He had witnessed a great deal of the hardships of the system of Slavery, and he had quite enough intelligence to portray the horrors thereof in very vivid colors. It was the auction-block horror that first prompted him to seek freedom. While thinking how he would manage to get away safely, his wife and children were ever present in his mind. He felt as a husband should towards his 'wife Betsy,' and likewise loved his 'children, Walter and Mary', but these belonged to another man, who lived some distance in the country... he decided that it would not be best to break the secret to his poor wife and children, but to get off to Canada, and afterwards to try and see what he could do for their deliverance.

The Underground Rail Road: A Record
(The True Story of James Burrell, pages 148-149)

• • • • • • •

The Patrol System Survived

With the war lost, Southern whites' fears of African Americans increased in 1865 due to reconstruction governments that were oppressive to the South. Even though Slavery and patrols were legally ended, the patrol system still survived. Almost immediately in the aftermath of the war, informal patrols sprang into action. Later, city and rural police squads, along with the help of Union army officers, revived patrolling practices among free men. During the post-Civil War Reconstruction period of 1865–1877, old-style patrol methods resurfaced and were enforced by postwar Southern police officers and also by organizations such as the Ku Klux Klan.

https://en.wikipedia.org/wiki/Slave_patrol

"We Are the Voice of One" Prayer Declaration
(Declare Aloud)

We are the Voice of One that crieth in [city and state]: "Prepare Ye the way of the Lord!

Make straight in [city] a highway for our God; Every valley in [city] shall be exalted; And every mountain and hill in [city] shall be brought low. The crooked places in [city] shall be made straight; And the rough places shall be made smooth; And the glory of the Lord shall be revealed in [city and state]; And all of [city] and all nations shall see it together; for the mouth of the Lord has spoken it!"

Heavenly Father, we both claim and proclaim your prophecy that is written in Genesis 15: "Your descendants will be strangers in a foreign land; they will be slaves there and will be treated cruelly for four hundred years. But I will punish the nation that enslaves them, and when they leave that foreign land, they will take great wealth with them, "Heavenly Father, make us one, just as You and the Lord Jesus are One! Heavenly Father, increase our numbers and gather Your people to pray! Let the Holy Spirit move freely, and the zeal of the Lord of Hosts shall accomplish it! In Jesus' name! Amen!

Offer a Closing Prayer to God
And as you pray....

- Consider the prayers of the enslaved as they lay on the slave ship, stored chained together and stored like cargo for months on an unknown journey that was thousands of miles long. The bodies of the enslaved who died in the Middle Passage were thrown in Atlantic Ocean.

- Imagine the prayers of the enslaved as they fled for freedom, following the North Star despite threats of lynching, beating, mutation, and death.

- Call out the names of the enslaved who were highlighted in today's reading from *The Underground Rail Road* and remember their descendants who still experience systemic racial oppression caused by social engineering.

Day 17

"Daniel fled from Norfolk, Va., where he had been owned by the late Richard Scott. Only a few days before Daniel escaped, his so-called owner was summoned to his last account. While ill, just before the close of his career, he often promised Daniel his freedom and also promised, if restored, that he would make amends for the past, by changing his ways of living. His son, who was very reckless, he would frequently allude to and declared, 'that he', the son, 'should not have his property.' These dying sentiments filled Daniel with great hopes that the day of his enslavement was nearly at an end. Unfortunately, however, death visited the old master, ere he had made provision for his slaves. At all events, no will was found. That he might not fall a prey to the reckless son, he felt, that he must nerve himself for a desperate struggle to obtain his freedom in some other way, by traveling on the Underground Rail Road… He was called upon in this trying hour to leave his wife with three children, but they were, fortunately, free."

The Underground Rail Road: A Record
(The True Story of Daniel Wiggins
alias Daniel Robinson, page 149)

• • • • • • •

The Network Supporting Slavery in America
Financial Institutions

America's second biggest bank, JP Morgan Chase, has made a rare apology for its subsidiaries' involvement in the slave trade 200 years ago, admitting that it accepted slaves as loan collateral and ended up owning several hundred.

The Wall Street heavyweight said parts of the business accepted thousands of slaves as collateral on loans made to plantation owners in the South in the early 19th century.

The banks sometimes took ownership of slaves when the plantation owners defaulted on loans.

Citizens' Bank and Canal Bank in Louisiana, both now part of JP Morgan, served plantations from the 1830s until the American civil war, which ended in 1865.

The company estimated that between 1831 and 1865 the two banks accepted approximately 13,000 slaves as collateral and ended up owning about 1,250 slaves.

https://www.theguardian.com/world/2005/jan/22/usa.davidteather

"We Are the Voice of One" Prayer Declaration
(Declare Aloud)

We are the Voice of One that crieth in [city and state]: "Prepare Ye the way of the Lord!

Make straight in [city] highway for our God; Every valley in [city] shall be exalted; And every mountain and hill in [city] shall be brought low. The crooked places in [city] shall be made straight; And the rough places shall be made smooth; And the glory of the Lord shall be revealed in [city and state]; And all of [city] and all nations shall see it together; for the mouth of the Lord has spoken it!"

Heavenly Father, we both claim and proclaim your prophecy that is written in Genesis 15: "Your descendants will be strangers in a foreign land; they will be slaves there and will be treated cruelly for **four hundred years**. But I will punish the nation that enslaves them, and when they leave that foreign land, they will take great wealth with them." Heavenly Father, make us one, just as You and the Lord Jesus are One! Heavenly Father, increase our numbers and gather Your people to pray! Let the Holy Spirit move freely, and the zeal of the Lord of Hosts shall accomplish it! In Jesus' name! Amen!

Offer a Closing Prayer to God
And as you pray....

- Consider the prayers of the enslaved as they lay on the slave ship, stored chained together and stored like cargo for months on an unknown journey that was thousands of miles long. The bodies of the enslaved who died in the Middle Passage were thrown in Atlantic Ocean.

- Imagine the prayers of the enslaved as they fled for freedom, following the North Star despite threats of lynching, beating, mutation, and death.

- Call out the names of the enslaved who were highlighted in today's reading from *The Underground Rail Road* and remember their descendants who still experience systemic racial oppression caused by social engineering.

Day 18

"Father and daughter were fortunate enough to escape together from Norfolk, Va. Harrison was just in the prime of life, forty years of age, stout made, good features, but in height was rather below medium…he alleged that he had been used hard. Harriet Ann was a well-grown girl of pleasant appearance, fourteen years of age…Harrison had been informed that his children were to be sold; to prevent this shocking fate, he was prompted to escape…While the records contain no definite account of other children, it is evident that there were others, but what became of them is not known."

The Underground Rail Road: A Record
(The True Story of Harrison Bell
and Daughter Harriet Ann, page 151)

· · · · · · ·

The Network Supporting Slavery in America
Supporters in the North and the South

"Northern shippers also profited handsomely after 1808 in the brisk interstate transfer in slaves that saw some one million bondsmen transferred by sea as well as land from the Upper to the Lower South between 1810 and 1860. Thus it was not in New Orleans but Providence that some of the state's most prosperous and influential citizens gathered at what the local newspaper described as "a very numerous and respectable" meeting, on Nov. 2, 1835, to unanimously endorse several resolutions condemning the actions of recently formed anti-slavery societies in the free states, declaring "coercive measures for the abolition of slavery" a "violation of the sacred rights of property." This proclamation was altogether fitting. Rhode Island had sent more than twice as many ships to Africa for slaves than all of the other colonies or states combined, many of them as part of the infamous Triangular Trade in which New England rum was exchanged for African slaves who then endured the horrific "middle passage" that brought them to the auction blocks of southern or Caribbean ports. Across the region, a sizable workforce was also employed in building the vessels requisite to these activities. Although slavery was said to be the "peculiar institution" of the South, even the loftiest families of old Boston were tapped into the enormous, far reaching stream of wealth it produced."

http://time.com/4274901/slavery-traces-history/

"We Are the Voice of One" Prayer Declaration
(Declare Aloud)

We are the Voice of One that crieth in [city and state]: "Prepare Ye the way of the Lord!

Make straight in [city] highway for our God; Every valley in [city] shall be exalted; And every mountain and hill in [city] shall be brought low. The crooked places in [city] shall be made straight; And the rough places shall be made smooth; And the glory of the Lord shall be revealed in [city and state]; And all of [city] and all nations shall see it together; for the mouth of the Lord has spoken it!"

Heavenly Father, we both claim and proclaim your prophecy that is written in Genesis 15: "Your descendants will be strangers in a foreign land; they will be slaves there and will be treated cruelly for **four hundred years**. But I will punish the nation that enslaves them, and when they leave that foreign land, they will take great wealth with them." Heavenly Father, make us one, just as You and the Lord Jesus are One! Heavenly Father, increase our numbers and gather Your people to pray! Let the Holy Spirit move freely, and the zeal of the Lord of Hosts shall accomplish it! In Jesus' name! Amen!

Offer a Closing Prayer to God
And as you pray....

- Consider the prayers of the enslaved as they lay on the slave ship, stored chained together and stored like cargo for months on an unknown journey that was thousands of miles long. The bodies of the enslaved who died in the Middle Passage were thrown in Atlantic Ocean.

- Imagine the prayers of the enslaved as they fled for freedom, following the North Star despite threats of lynching, beating, mutation, and death.

- Call out the names of the enslaved who were highlighted in today's reading from *The Underground Rail Road* and remember their descendants who still experience systemic racial oppression caused by social engineering.

Day 19

"Daniel was only about twenty, just at a capital age to make a bold strike for freedom...Hon. Charles J. Fortner, M.C. was the reputed owner of this young fugitive...Daniel was placed in the employ of a farmer, by the name of Adam Quigley...he declared that Quigley was a 'very mean man', one for whom he had no respect whatever...While he was yet so young, he had pretty clear views with regard to Slavery, and remembered with feelings of deep indignation, how his father had been sold when he himself was a boy, just as a horse might have been sold; and how his mother was dragging her chains in Slavery, up to the hour he fled. Thus, in company with his two companions he was prepared for any sacrifice."

The Underground Rail Road: A Record
(The True Story of Daniel David alias David Smith, page 151)

· · · · · · ·

The Network Supporting Slavery in America
Supporters in the North and the South

"There are very many economic links between the southern plantation complex and the development of American and global capitalism, involving trade, industry, banking, insurance, shipping, and other industries. The most prominent link developed around cotton.

As you know, the cotton industry was crucial to the world-altering Industrial Revolution as it first unfolded in Great Britain and then spread from there to other parts of the world, including the northern states of the Union. Until 1861, until the American Civil War, almost all cotton used in industrial production was grown by enslaved workers in the southern parts of the United States. Slavery thus played a very important role in supplying an essential raw material for industrial production."

https://www.forbes.com/sites/hbsworkingknowledge/2017/05/03/the-clear-connection-between-slavery-and-american-capitalism/#7c9839fc7bd3

"We Are the Voice of One" Prayer Declaration
(Declare Aloud)

We are the Voice of One that crieth in [city and state]: "Prepare Ye the way of the Lord!

Make straight in [city] a highway for our God; Every valley in [city] shall be exalted; And every mountain and hill in [city] shall be brought low. The crooked places in [city] shall be made straight; And the rough places shall be made smooth; And the glory of the Lord shall be revealed in [city and state]; And all of [city] and all nations shall see it together; for the mouth of the Lord has spoken it!"

Heavenly Father, we both claim and proclaim your prophecy that is written in Genesis 15: "Your descendants will be strangers in a foreign land; they will be slaves there and will be treated cruelly for **four hundred years**. But I will punish the nation that enslaves them, and when they leave that foreign land, they will take great wealth with them." Heavenly Father, make us one, just as You and the Lord Jesus are One! Heavenly Father, increase our numbers and gather Your people to pray! Let the Holy Spirit move freely, and the zeal of the Lord of Hosts shall accomplish it! In Jesus' name! Amen!

Offer a Closing Prayer to God
And as you pray....

- Consider the prayers of the enslaved as they lay on the slave ship, stored chained together and stored like cargo for months on an unknown journey that was thousands of miles long. The bodies of the enslaved who died in the Middle Passage were thrown in Atlantic Ocean.

- Imagine the prayers of the enslaved as they fled for freedom, following the North Star despite threats of lynching, beating, mutation, and death.

- Call out the names of the enslaved who were highlighted in today's reading from *The Underground Rail Road* and remember their descendants who still experience systemic racial oppression caused by social engineering.

Day 20

"Sarah and her daughter, nine years of age were held in service by the Rev. A.D. Pollock, a resident of Wilmington, Del. Until about nine months before she escaped from the Reverend gentleman, she was owned by Mrs. Elizabeth Lee of Fauquier Co., Va., who had moved with Sarah to Wilmington...it was owing to ill treatment from her mistress that Sarah 'took out' with her child."

The Underground Rail Road: A Record
(The True Story of Sarah Smith alias Mildreth Page, page 153)

· · · · · · ·

The Network Supporting Slavery in America
Supporters in the North and the South

"Yet there were further links: British and later U.S. capital financed the expansion of the slavery complex in the American South. Advancing credit was essential for southern planters to be able to purchase land and labor. Northern merchants, moreover, organized the shipment of cotton into global markets.

And of course northern manufacturers, along with their European counterparts, supplied plantations in the South with tools, textiles, and other goods that were necessary to maintain the plantation regime. Plantation slavery, far from being a retrograde system on its way to being ousted by industrial capitalism, saw a second flourishing in the 19th century in the wake of the industrial revolution. And in the United States, cotton was central to that "second slavery."

https://www.forbes.com/sites/hbsworkingknowledge/2017/05/03/the-clear-connection-between-slavery-and-american-capitalism/#7c9839fc7bd3

"We Are the Voice of One" Prayer Declaration
(Declare Aloud)

We are the Voice of One that crieth in [city and state]: "Prepare Ye the way of the Lord!

Make straight in [city] a highway for our God; Every valley in [city] shall be exalted; And every mountain and hill in [city] shall be brought low. The crooked places in [city] shall be made straight; And the rough places shall be made smooth; And the glory of the Lord shall be revealed in [city and state]; And all of [city] and all nations shall see it together; for the mouth of the Lord has spoken it!"

Heavenly Father, we both claim and proclaim your prophecy that is written in Genesis 15: "Your descendants will be strangers in a foreign land; they will be slaves there and will be treated cruelly for **four hundred years**. But I will punish the nation that enslaves them, and when they leave that foreign land, they will take great wealth with them." Heavenly Father, make us one, just as You and the Lord Jesus are One! Heavenly Father, increase our numbers and gather Your people to pray! Let the Holy Spirit move freely, and the zeal of the Lord of Hosts shall accomplish it! In Jesus' name! Amen!

Offer a Closing Prayer to God
And as you pray....

- Consider the prayers of the enslaved as they lay on the slave ship, stored chained together and stored like cargo for months on an unknown journey that was thousands of miles long. The bodies of the enslaved who died in the Middle Passage were thrown in Atlantic Ocean.

- Imagine the prayers of the enslaved as they fled for freedom, following the North Star despite threats of lynching, beating, mutation, and death.

- Call out the names of the enslaved who were highlighted in today's reading from *The Underground Rail Road* and remember their descendants who still experience systemic racial oppression caused by social engineering.

Day 21

"George was a spare-built man, about twenty-five years of age, quite dark, but had considerable intelligence. He could read and write very well, but how he acquired these arts is not known. It was only by the most indomitable resolution and perseverance, that Freeland threw off the yoke. Capt. John Pollard of Petersburg, Va., held George to service. As a Slave-holder, Pollard belongs to that class, who did not believe in granting favors to Slaves. On the contrary, he was practically in favor of wringing every drop of blood from their bodies. In testifying against his master, George used very strong language. He declared that Pollard "thought no more of his servants than if they had been dogs. He was very mean...In leaving the land of Slave auctions, whips and chains, he was obliged to leave his mother and father and two brothers in Petersburg."

The Underground Rail Road: A Record
(The True Story of George W. Freeland, pages 153-154)

· · · · · · ·

The International Network Supporting Slavery in America *Britain*

The thriving British economy after 1660 was made possible mainly because of Britain's financial institutions. Trading houses, insurance companies and banks emerged to underpin Britain's overseas trade and empire. The expansion of overseas trade, especially in the Atlantic, relied on credit, and bills of credit (like modern travellers cheques), which were at the heart of the slave trade. Similarly, the maritime insurance, which was focused at Lloyds of London, thrived on the Atlantic slave trade.

There were no banks in the City until the mid-17th century, and even a century later, banking was under-developed outside London. But slave traders and planters badly needed credit. A slave voyage from Liverpool to Africa then on to the Caribbean, before heading home, could take 18 months. And each point of the trade - buying and selling Africans, buying and importing produce (mainly sugar) cultivated using the labour of enslaved people - involved credit arrangements. Merchants and traders in London, Bristol and Liverpool, bought the planters' produce, so in effect, British merchants became the bankers of the slave trade.

Provincial banking emerged in the 18th century because of the need for credit in the long-distance Atlantic slave trade. For example, Liverpool merchants involved in slave trading later formed Heywoods Bank, which eventually became part of Barclays Bank. Other modern banking names, such as Lloyds, emerged in this way and inevitably had links to the Atlantic slave trade. The Bank of England was also involved. When it was set up in 1694, it underpinned the whole system of commercial credit, and its wealthy City members, from the governor down, were often men whose fortunes had been made wholly or partly in the slave trade. The Bank of England stabilised the national finances, and enabled the state to wage its major wars of the 18th century. These wars were aimed at securing and safeguarding overseas possessions, including the slave colonies, and to finance the military and naval means that protected the Atlantic slave routes and the plantation economies."

http://www.bbc.co.uk/history/british/abolition/building_britain_gallery_02.shtml

"We Are the Voice of One" Prayer Declaration
(Declare Aloud)

We are the Voice of One that crieth in [city and state]: "Prepare Ye the way of the Lord!

Make straight in [city] a highway for our God; Every valley in [city] shall be exalted; And every mountain and hill in [city] shall be brought low. The crooked places in [city] shall be made straight; And the rough places shall be made smooth; And the glory of the Lord shall be revealed in [city and state]; And all of [city] and all nations shall see it together; for the mouth of the Lord has spoken it!"

Heavenly Father, we both claim and proclaim your prophecy that is written in Genesis 15: "Your descendants will be strangers in a foreign land; they will be slaves there and will be treated cruelly for **four hundred years**. But I will punish the nation that enslaves them, and when they leave that foreign land, they will take great wealth with them." Heavenly Father, make us one, just as You and the Lord Jesus are One! Heavenly Father, increase our numbers and gather Your people to pray! Let the Holy Spirit move freely, and the zeal of the Lord of Hosts shall accomplish it! In Jesus' name! Amen!

Offer a Closing Prayer to God
And as you pray....

- Consider the prayers of the enslaved as they lay on the slave ship, stored chained together and stored like cargo for months on an unknown journey that was thousands of miles long. The bodies of the enslaved who died in the Middle Passage were thrown in Atlantic Ocean.

- Imagine the prayers of the enslaved as they fled for freedom, following the North Star despite threats of lynching, beating, mutation, and death.

- Call out the names of the enslaved who were highlighted in today's reading from *The Underground Rail Road* and remember their descendants who still experience systemic racial oppression caused by social engineering.

Day 22

"John fled from South Carolina. In this hot-bed of Slavery he labored and suffered up to the age of thirty-two. For a length of time before he escaped, his burdens were intolerable; but he could see no way to rid himself of them, except by flight. Nor was he by any means certain that an effort in this direction would prove successful. In planning the route which he should take to travel North he decided, that if success was for him, his best chance would be to wend his ways through North Carolina and Virginia. Nor that he hoped to find friends or helpers in these States. He had heard enough of the cruelties of Slavery in these regions to convince him, that if he should be caught, there would be no sympathy or mercy shown. Nevertheless, the irons were piercing him so severely, that he felt constrained to try his luck, let the consequences be what they might, and so he set out for freedom or death. Mountains of difficulties, and months of suffering and privations by land and water, in the woods, and swamps of North Carolina and Virginia, were before him, as his experience in traveling proved. But the hope of final victory and his daily sufferings before he started, kept him from faltering, even when starvation and death seemed to be staring him in the face. For several months he was living in dens and caves of the earth."

The Underground Rail Road: A Record
(The True Story of John Hall, alias John Simpson, page 154)

• • • • • • •

United States v. Reese

This was the Supreme Court's first voting rights case under the Fifteenth Amendment and the Enforcement Act of 1870. A Kentucky electoral official had refused to register an African American's vote in a municipal election and was indicted under two sections of the 1871 Act: Section 1 required that administrative preliminaries to elections be conducted without regard to race, color, or previous condition of servitude; Section 2 forbade wrongful refusal to register votes where a prerequisite step "required as foresaid" had been omitted.

The Court held that the Fifteenth Amendment did not confer the right of suffrage, but it prohibited exclusion from voting on racial grounds. The justices invalidated the operative Section 3 of the Enforcement Act since it did not repeat the amendment's words about race, color, and servitude. They ruled that the section exceeded the scope of the Fifteenth Amendment. This ruling was the grounds for which the Ku Klux Klan was established, as it provided white southerners with legal reassurance.

https://en.wikipedia.org/wiki/United_States_v._Reese

"We Are the Voice of One" Prayer Declaration
(Declare Aloud)

We are the Voice of One that crieth in [city and state]: "Prepare Ye the way of the Lord!

Make straight in [city] a highway for our God; Every valley in [city] shall be exalted; And every mountain and hill in [city] shall be brought low. The crooked places in [city] shall be made straight; And the rough places shall be made smooth; And the glory of the Lord shall be revealed in [city and state]; And all of [city] and all nations shall see it together; for the mouth of the Lord has spoken it!"

Heavenly Father, we both claim and proclaim your prophecy that is written in Genesis 15: "Your descendants will be strangers in a foreign land; they will be slaves there and will be treated cruelly for **four hundred years**. But I will punish the nation that enslaves them, and when they leave that foreign land, they will take great wealth with them." Heavenly Father, make us one, just as You and the Lord Jesus are One! Heavenly Father, increase our numbers and gather Your people to pray! Let the Holy Spirit move freely, and the zeal of the Lord of Hosts shall accomplish it! In Jesus' name! Amen!

Offer a Closing Prayer to God
And as you pray....

- Consider the prayers of the enslaved as they lay on the slave ship, stored chained together and stored like cargo for months on an

unknown journey that was thousands of miles long. The bodies of the enslaved who died in the Middle Passage were thrown in Atlantic Ocean.

- Imagine the prayers of the enslaved as they fled for freedom, following the North Star despite threats of lynching, beating, mutation, and death.

- Call out the names of the enslaved who were highlighted in today's reading from The Underground Rail Road and remember their descendants who still experience systemic racial oppression caused by social engineering.

Day 23

"Robert and his wife, Eliza: In the majority of cases, in order to effect the escape of either, sad separations between husbands and wives were unavoidable. Fortunately, it was not so in this case. In journeying from the house of bondage, Robert and his wife were united both in sympathies and struggles. On August 2d, 1855, Robert Jones and wife, arrived from Petersburg, Va. Robert is about thirty-five, chestnut color, medium size, of good manners, intelligent, had been owned by Thomas N. Lee, 'a very hard man.' Robert left because he 'wanted his liberty — always had from a boy.' Eliza, his wife, is about forty years of age, chestnut color, nice-looking and well-dressed. She belonged to Eliza H. Ritchie, who was called a 'moderate woman' towards her slaves. Notwithstanding the limited space occupied in noting them on the record book, the Committee regarded them as being among the most worthy and brave travelers passing over the Underground Rail Road, and felt well satisfied that such specimens of humanity would do credit in Canada, not only to themselves, but to their race."

The Underground Rail Road: A Record
(The True Story of Robert Jones and Wife, Eliza, page 175)

· · · · · · ·

The Results from the *United States v. Reese* Ruling

Due to this ruling, states began to develop means to exclude blacks from voting while keeping within the constraints of the 14th Amendment. They adopted such devices as poll taxes (which many poor black and white sharecroppers, who lived on credit, did not have ready cash to pay); literacy tests, subjectively administered by white election officials, who tended in practice to exclude even educated blacks which is often very rare; grandfather clauses, which admitted voters whose grandfathers had voted as of a certain date, which also excluded blacks; and more restrictive residency requirements, which disqualified people who had to move to follow work. As these measures were challenged in court, beginning with Mississippi's new constitution in 1890 that included them, the Supreme Court upheld their use, as they were required of all voters. The court did not believe it had a role in overseeing the practice of these measures, which white Democrats quickly used to disfranchise most black voters across the South. Through 1910, all the former Confederate states passed new constitutions or amendments to achieve disfranchisement.

https://en.wikipedia.org/wiki/United_States_v._Reese

"We Are the Voice of One" Prayer Declaration
(Declare Aloud)

We are the Voice of One that crieth in [city and state]: "Prepare Ye the way of the Lord!

Make straight in [city] a highway for our God; Every valley in [city] shall be exalted; And every mountain and hill in [city] shall be brought low. The crooked places in [city] shall be made straight; And the rough places shall be made smooth; And the glory of the Lord shall be revealed in [city and state]; And all of [city] and all nations shall see it together; for the mouth of the Lord has spoken it!"

Heavenly Father, we both claim and proclaim your prophecy that is written in Genesis 15: "Your descendants will be strangers in a foreign land; they will be slaves there and will be treated cruelly for **four hundred years**. But I will punish the nation that enslaves them, and when they leave that foreign land, they will take great wealth with them." Heavenly Father, make us one, just as You and the Lord Jesus are One! Heavenly Father, increase our numbers and gather Your people to pray! Let the Holy Spirit move freely, and the zeal of the Lord of Hosts shall accomplish it! In Jesus' name! Amen!

Offer a Closing Prayer to God
And as you pray....

- Consider the prayers of the enslaved as they lay on the slave ship, stored chained together and stored like cargo for months on an unknown journey that was thousands of miles long. The bodies of the enslaved who died in the Middle Passage were thrown in Atlantic Ocean.

- Imagine the prayers of the enslaved as they fled for freedom, following the North Star despite threats of lynching, beating, mutation, and death.

- Call out the names of the enslaved who were highlighted in today's reading from *The Underground Rail Road* and remember their descendants who still experience systemic racial oppression caused by social engineering.

Day 24 _____

"Laura arrived from Louisville, Kentucky. She had been owned by a widow woman named Lewis, but as lately as the previous March her mistress died, leaving her slaves and other property to be divided among her heirs. As this would necessitate a sale of the slaves, Laura determined not to be on hand when the selling day came, so she took time by forelock and left...She was about twenty-five years, quite stout, of mixed blood, and intelligent…She left her mother, one brother, and one sister in Louisville."

The Underground Rail Road: A Record
(The True Story of Laura Lewis, page 187)

· · · · · · ·

The Lynching of Mary Turner
(c. 1885 – 19 May 1918)

Mary was a young, married black woman and mother of two who was lynched by a white mob in Lowndes County, Georgia, for having protested the lynching death of her husband Hazel "Hayes" Turner the day before in Brooks County. She was eight months pregnant, and her unborn child also was brutally murdered. They were followed by the murders of eleven more black men by a white mob in Brooks and neighboring Lowndes counties during a manhunt and lynching rampage.

Following the lynchings, more than 500 black residents fled the area, although whites threatened to kill black workers who tried to leave. The lynching murders of Hayes and Mary Turner, and several other blacks, caused a brief national outcry. They were highlighted in the NAACP's campaigns for Congress to pass federal anti-lynching legislation.

https://en.wikipedia.org/wiki/May_1918_lynchings

"We Are the Voice of One" Prayer Declaration
(Declare Aloud)

We are the Voice of One that crieth in [city and state]: "Prepare Ye the way of the Lord!

Make straight in [city] a highway for our God; Every valley in [city] shall be exalted; And every mountain and hill in [city] shall be brought low. The crooked places in [city] shall be made straight; And the rough places shall be made smooth; And the glory of the Lord shall be revealed in [city and state]; And all of [city] and all nations shall see it together; for the mouth of the Lord has spoken it!"

Heavenly Father, we both claim and proclaim your prophecy that is written in Genesis 15: "Your descendants will be strangers in a foreign land; they will be slaves there and will be treated cruelly for **four hundred years**. But I will punish the nation that enslaves them, and when they leave that foreign land, they will take great wealth with them." Heavenly Father, make us one, just as You and the Lord Jesus are One! Heavenly Father, increase our numbers and gather Your people to pray! Let the Holy Spirit move freely, and the zeal of the Lord of Hosts shall accomplish it! In Jesus' name! Amen!

Offer a Closing Prayer to God
And as you pray....

- Consider the prayers of the enslaved as they lay on the slave ship, stored chained together and stored like cargo for months on an unknown journey that was thousands of miles long. The bodies of the enslaved who died in the Middle Passage were thrown in Atlantic Ocean.

- Imagine the prayers of the enslaved as they fled for freedom, following the North Star despite threats of lynching, beating, mutation, and death.

- Call out the names of the enslaved who were highlighted in today's reading from *The Underground Rail Road* and remember their descendants who still experience systemic racial oppression caused by social engineering.

Day 25 _____

"Of all the passengers who had hitherto arrived with bruised and mangled bodies received at the hands of slave-holders, none brought a back so shamefully lacerated by the lash as Thomas Madden. Not a single spot had been exempted from the excoriating cow-hide. A most bloody picture did the broad back and shoulders of Thomas present to the eye as he bared his wounds for inspection. While it was sad to think, that millions of men, women, and children throughout the South were liable to just such brutal outrages as Thomas had received, it was a satisfaction to think, that this outrage had made a freeman of him. He was only twenty-two years of age, but that punishment convinced him that he was fully old enough to leave such a master as E. Ray, who had almost murdered him."

The Underground Rail Road: A Record
(The True Story of Thomas Madden, page 189)

· · · · · · ·

Racial Segregation in the United States

An African-American historian, Marvin Dunn, described segregation in Miami, Florida, about 1950:

My mother shopped there [Burdine's Department Store], but she was not allowed to try on clothes or to return clothes. Blacks were not allowed to use the elevator or eat at the lunch counter. All the white stores were similar in this regard. The Greyhound Bus Station had separate waiting rooms and toilets for blacks and whites. Blacks could not eat at the counter in the bus station. The first black police officers for the city had been hired in 1947…but they could not arrest white people. My parents were registered as Republicans until the 1950s because they were not allowed to join the Democrat Party before 1947.

https://en.wikipedia.org/wiki/Racial_segregation_in_the_United_States

"We Are the Voice of One" Prayer Declaration
(Declare Aloud)

We are the Voice of One that crieth in [city and state]: "Prepare Ye the way of the Lord!

Make straight in [city] a highway for our God; Every valley in [city] shall be exalted; And every mountain and hill in [city] shall be brought low. The crooked places in [city] shall be made straight; And the rough places shall be made smooth; And the glory of the Lord shall be revealed in [city and state]; And all of [city] and all nations shall see it together; for the mouth of the Lord has spoken it!"

Heavenly Father, we both claim and proclaim your prophecy that is written in Genesis 15: "Your descendants will be strangers in a foreign land; they will be slaves there and will be treated cruelly for **four hundred years**. But I will punish the nation that enslaves them, and when they leave that foreign land, they will take great wealth with them." Heavenly Father, make us one, just as You and the Lord Jesus are One! Heavenly Father, increase our numbers and gather Your people to pray! Let the Holy Spirit move freely, and the zeal of the Lord of Hosts shall accomplish it! In Jesus' name! Amen!

Offer a Closing Prayer to God
And as you pray....

- Consider the prayers of the enslaved as they lay on the slave ship, stored chained together and stored like cargo for months on an unknown journey that was thousands of miles long. The bodies of the enslaved who died in the Middle Passage were thrown in Atlantic Ocean.

- Imagine the prayers of the enslaved as they fled for freedom, following the North Star despite threats of lynching, beating, mutation, and death.

- Call out the names of the enslaved who were highlighted in today's reading from *The Underground Rail Road* and remember their descendants who still experience systemic racial oppression caused by social engineering.

Day 26 _____

"Up to the age of thirty-give "Pete" had worn the yoke steadily, if not patiently under William S. Matthews, of Oak Hall, near Temperanceville, in the State of Virginia...the man to whom he 'was hired, George Matthews, was a very cruel man.' One day, a short while before Pete 'took out', an ox broke into the truck patch, and helped himself to choice delicacies...Peter's attention being directed to the ox...he gave him what he considered proper chastisement, according to the mischief he had done. At this liberty taken by Pete, the master became furious. 'He got his gun and threatened to shoot him,'...'He took out a large dirk-knife, and attempted to stab me, but I kept out of his way,' said Pete. Nevertheless, the violence of the master did not abate until he had beaten Peter over the head and body till he was weary, inflicting severe injuries. A great change was at once wrought in Peter's mind. He was now ready to adopt any plan that mighty hold out the least encouragement to escape...."

The Underground Rail Road: A Record
(The True Story of Pete Matthews alias Samuel Sparrows,
pages 189-190)

• • • • • • •

Redlining

In the 1960s, sociologist John McKnight coined the term "redlining" to describe the discriminatory practice of identifying areas where banks would avoid investments based on community demographics. During the heyday of redlining, the areas most frequently discriminated against were black inner city neighborhoods. For example, in Atlanta in the 1980s, a Pulitzer Prize-winning series of articles by investigative reporter Bill Dedman showed that banks would often lend to lower-income whites but not to middle-income or upper-income blacks.

https://en.wikipedia.org/wiki/Redlining

"We Are the Voice of One" Prayer Declaration
(Declare Aloud)

We are the Voice of One that crieth in [city and state]: "Prepare Ye the way of the Lord!

Make straight in [city] a highway for our God; Every valley in [city] shall be exalted; And every mountain and hill in [city] shall be brought low. The crooked places in [city] shall be made straight; And the rough places shall be made smooth; And the glory of the Lord shall be revealed in [city and state]; And all of [city] and all nations shall see it together; for the mouth of the Lord has spoken it!"

Heavenly Father, we both claim and proclaim your prophecy that is written in Genesis 15: "Your descendants will be strangers in a foreign land; they will be slaves there and will be treated cruelly for **four hundred years**. But I will punish the nation that enslaves them, and when they leave that foreign land, they will take great wealth with them." Heavenly Father, make us one, just as You and the Lord Jesus are One! Heavenly Father, increase our numbers and gather Your people to pray! Let the Holy Spirit move freely, and the zeal of the Lord of Hosts shall accomplish it! In Jesus' name! Amen!

Offer a Closing Prayer to God
And as you pray....

- Consider the prayers of the enslaved as they lay on the slave ship, stored chained together and stored like cargo for months on an unknown journey that was thousands of miles long. The bodies of the enslaved who died in the Middle Passage were thrown in Atlantic Ocean.

- Imagine the prayers of the enslaved as they fled for freedom, following the North Star despite threats of lynching, beating, mutation, and death.

- Call out the names of the enslaved who were highlighted in today's reading from *The Underground Rail Road* and remember their descendants who still experience systemic racial oppression caused by social engineering.

Day 27

"December 29th, 1854 - *Moses* (Harriet Tubman) arrives with six passengers: John Chase, Benjamin Ross, Henry Ross, Peter Jackson, Jane Kane, and Robert Ross...Harriet Tubman had been their "Moses," but not in the sense that Andrew Johnson was the 'Moses of the colored people'. She had faithfully gone down into Egypt, and had delivered these six bondmen by her own heroism. Harriet was a woman of no pretensions, indeed, a more ordinary specimen of humanity could hardly be found among the most unfortunate-looking farm hands of the South. Yet, in point of courage, shrewdness and disinterested exertions to rescue her fellow-men, by making personal visit to Maryland among the slaves, she was without her equal. Her success was wonderful. Time and again she made successful visits to Maryland on the Underground Rail Road, and would be absent for weeks, at a time, running daily risks while making preparations for herself and passengers. Great fears were entertained for her safety, but she seemed wholly devoid of personal fear...She had a very short and pointed rule or law of her own, which implied death to any who talked of giving out and going back...After having once enlisted, 'they had to go through or die.' Of course Harriet was supreme, and her followers generally had full faith in her, and would back up any word she might utter. So when she said to them that 'a live runaway could do great harm by going back, but that a dead one could tell no secrets,' she was sure to have obedience. Therefore, none had to die as traitors on the 'middle passage.'"

The Underground Rail Road: A Record
(The True Story of "Moses" aka Harriet Tubman, pages 190-191)

· · · · · · ·

Educational Oppression

The enslavement of African Americans removed the access to education for generations. Once the legal abolishment of slavery was enacted, racial stigma remained. Social, economic, and political barriers held blacks in a position of subordination. Although legally African Americans had the ability to be learning how to read and write, they were often prohibited from attending schools with White students. This form of segregation is often referred to as de jure segregation. The schools that allowed African American students to attend often lacked financial support, thus providing inadequate educational skills for their students. Freedmen's schools existed but they focused on maintaining African Americans in servitude, not an enriching academic prosperity. The United States then experienced legal separation in schools between whites and blacks. Schools were supposed to receive equal resources but there was an undoubted inequality. It was not until 1968 that Black students in the South had universal secondary education.

https://en.wikipedia.org/wiki/Educational_inequality

"We Are the Voice of One" Prayer Declaration
(Declare Aloud)

We are the Voice of One that crieth in [city and state]: "Prepare Ye the way of the Lord!

Make straight in [city] a highway for our God; Every valley in [city] shall be exalted; And every mountain and hill in [city] shall be brought low. The crooked places in [city] shall be made straight; And the rough places shall be made smooth; And the glory of the Lord shall be revealed in [city and state]; And all of [city] and all nations shall see it together; for the mouth of the Lord has spoken it!"

Heavenly Father, we both claim and proclaim your prophecy that is written in Genesis 15: "Your descendants will be strangers in a foreign land; they will be slaves there and will be treated cruelly for **four hundred years**. But I will punish the nation that enslaves them, and when they leave that foreign land, they will take great wealth with them." Heavenly Father, make us one, just as You and the Lord Jesus are One! Heavenly Father, increase our numbers and gather Your people to pray! Let the Holy Spirit move freely, and the zeal of the Lord of Hosts shall accomplish it! In Jesus' name! Amen!

Offer a Closing Prayer to God
And as you pray....

- Consider the prayers of the enslaved as they lay on the slave ship, stored chained together and stored like cargo for months on an unknown journey that was thousands of miles long. The bodies of the enslaved who died in the Middle Passage were thrown in Atlantic Ocean.

- Imagine the prayers of the enslaved as they fled for freedom, following the North Star despite threats of lynching, beating, mutation, and death.

- Call out the names of the enslaved who were highlighted in today's reading from *The Underground Rail Road* and remember their descendants who still experience systemic racial oppression caused by social engineering.

Day 28

"John Wesley Gibson represented himself to be not only the slave, but also the son of William Y. Day, of Taylor's Mount, Maryland. The faintest shade of colored blood was hardly discernible in this passenger. He relied wholly on his father's white blood to secure him freedom. Having resolved to serve no longer as a slave, he concluded to 'hold up his head and put on airs.' He reached Baltimore safely without being discovered or suspected of being on the Underground Rail Road...Here he tried for the first time to pass for white; the attempt proved a success beyond his expectation. Although a man of only twenty-eight years of age, he was foreman of his master's farm, but he was not particularly favored in any way on this account. His master and father endeavored to hold the reins very tightly upon him. Not even allowing him the privilege of visiting around on neighboring plantations. Perhaps the master thought the family likeness was rather too discernible. John believed that on this account all privileges were denied him, and he resolved to escape. His mother, Harriet, and sister, Frances, were named as near kin whom he had left behind."

The Underground Rail Road: A Record
(The True Story of John Wesley Gibson, pages 193-194)

• • • • • • •

The New Jim Crow

The New Jim Crow: Mass Incarceration in the Age of Colorblindness is a book by Michelle Alexander, a civil rights litigator and legal scholar. The book discusses race-related issues specific to African-American males and mass incarceration in the United States. Though the conventional point of view holds that racial discrimination mostly ended with the civil rights movement reforms of the 1960s, Alexander posits that the U.S. criminal justice system uses the War on Drugs as a primary tool for enforcing traditional, as well as new, modes of discrimination and oppression. These new modes of racism have led to not only the highest rate of incarceration in the world, but also a disproportionately large rate of imprisonment for African-American men. Were present trends to continue, Alexander writes, the United States will imprison one-third of its African American population. When combined with the fact that whites are more likely to commit drug crimes…, the issue becomes clear for Alexander: "The primary targets of [the penal system's] control can be defined largely by race."

https://en.wikipedia.org/wiki/The_New_Jim_Crow

"We Are the Voice of One" Prayer Declaration
(Declare Aloud)

We are the Voice of One that crieth in [city and state]: "Prepare Ye the way of the Lord!

Make straight in [city] a highway for our God; Every valley in [city] shall be exalted; And every mountain and hill in [city] shall be brought low. The crooked places in [city] shall be made straight; And the rough places shall be made smooth; And the glory of the Lord shall be revealed in [city and state]; And all of [city] and all nations shall see it together; for the mouth of the Lord has spoken it!"

Heavenly Father, we both claim and proclaim your prophecy that is written in Genesis 15: "Your descendants will be strangers in a foreign land; they will be slaves there and will be treated cruelly for **four hundred years**. But I will punish the nation that enslaves them, and when they leave that foreign land, they will take great wealth with them." Heavenly Father, make us one, just as You and the Lord Jesus are One! Heavenly Father, increase our numbers and gather Your people to pray! Let the Holy Spirit move freely, and the zeal of the Lord of Hosts shall accomplish it! In Jesus' name! Amen!

Offer a Closing Prayer to God
And as you pray....

- Consider the prayers of the enslaved as they lay on the slave ship, stored chained together and stored like cargo for months on an unknown journey that was thousands of miles long. The bodies of the enslaved who died in the Middle Passage were thrown in Atlantic Ocean.

- Imagine the prayers of the enslaved as they fled for freedom, following the North Star despite threats of lynching, beating, mutation, and death.

- Call out the names of the enslaved who were highlighted in today's reading from *The Underground Rail Road* and remember their descendants who still experience systemic racial oppression caused by social engineering.

Day 29 _____

"Harriet Shephard, the mother of five children, for whom she felt of course a mother's love, could not bear the thought of having her offspring compelled to wear the miserable yoke of Slavery, as she had been compelled to do. By her own personal experience, Harriet could very well judge what their fate would be when reaching man and womanhood. She declared that she had never received 'kind treatment'. It was not on this account, however, that she was prompted to escape…She was chiefly induced to make the bold effort to save her children from having to drag the chains of Slavery as she herself had done. Anna Maria, Edwin, Eliza Jane, Mary Ann, and John Henry were the names of the children for whom she was willing to make any sacrifice. They were young; and unable to walk, and she was penniless…Her rude intellect being considered, she was entitled to a great deal of credit for seizing the horses and carriages belonging to her master, as she did for the liberation of her children."

The Underground Rail Road: A Record
(The True Story of Harriet Shephard and Her Five Children, page 194)

• • • • • • •

Institutional Racism

The racial segregation and disparities in wealth between Caucasians and African-American people include legacies of historical policies. In the Social Security Act of 1935, agricultural workers and servants, most of whom were black, were excluded because key white southerners did not want governmental assistance to change the agrarian system. In the Wagner Act of 1935, "blacks were blocked by law from challenging the barriers to entry into the newly protected labor unions and securing the right to collective bargaining." In the National Housing Act of 1939, the property appraisal system tied property value and eligibility for government loans to race. The *1936 Underwriting Manual* used by the Federal Housing Administration to guide residential mortgages gave 20 percent weight to a neighborhood's protection, for example, zoning ordinances, deed restrictions, high speed traffic arteries, from adverse influences, such as infiltration of inharmonious racial groups. Thus, white-majority neighborhoods received the government's highest property value ratings, and white people were eligible for government loans and aid. Between 1934 and 1962, less than 2 percent of government-subsidized housing went to non-white people.

https://en.wikipedia.org/wiki/Institutional_racism

"We Are the Voice of One" Prayer Declaration
(Declare Aloud)

We are the Voice of One that crieth in [city and state]: "Prepare Ye the way of the Lord!

Make straight in [city] a highway for our God; Every valley in [city] shall be exalted; And every mountain and hill in [city] shall be brought low. The crooked places in [city] shall be made straight; And the rough places shall be made smooth; And the glory of the Lord shall be revealed in [city and state]; And all of [city] and all nations shall see it together; for the mouth of the Lord has spoken it!"

Heavenly Father, we both claim and proclaim your prophecy that is written in Genesis 15: "Your descendants will be strangers in a foreign land; they will be slaves there and will be treated cruelly for **four hundred years**. But I will punish the nation that enslaves them, and when they leave that foreign land, they will take great wealth with them." Heavenly Father, make us one, just as You and the Lord Jesus are One! Heavenly Father, increase our numbers and gather Your people to pray! Let the Holy Spirit move freely, and the zeal of the Lord of Hosts shall accomplish it! In Jesus' name! Amen!

Offer a Closing Prayer to God
And as you pray....

- Consider the prayers of the enslaved as they lay on the slave ship, stored chained together and stored like cargo for months on an unknown journey that was thousands of miles long. The bodies of the enslaved who died in the Middle Passage were thrown in Atlantic Ocean.

- Imagine the prayers of the enslaved as they fled for freedom, following the North Star despite threats of lynching, beating, mutation, and death.

- Call out the names of the enslaved who were highlighted in today's reading from The Underground Rail Road and remember their descendants who still experience systemic racial oppression caused by social engineering.

Day 30

"But few could tell of having been eye-witnesses to outrages more revolting and disgraceful than Washington Somlor. He arrived per steamer Pennsylvania (secreted), directly from Norfolk, Virginia, in 1855. He was thirty-two years of age — a man of medium size and quite intelligent. A merchant by the name of Smith owned Washington...Smith believed in selling, flogging, cobbing, paddling, and all other kinds of torture, by which he could inflict punishment in order to make the slaves feel his power. He thus tyrannized over about twenty-five head. Being naturally passionate, when in a brutal mood, he made his slaves suffer unmercifully. Said Washington, 'On one occasion, about two months before I was secreted, he had five of the slaves (some of them women) tied across a barrel, lashed with the cow-hide and then cobbed — this was a common practice.'

The Underground Rail Road: A Record
(The True Story of Washington Somlor alias James Moore, page 195)

· · · · · · ·

Institutional Racism

In 1968, the Fair Housing Act (FHA) was signed into law to eliminate the effects of state-sanctioned racial segregation. But it failed to change the status quo as the United States remained nearly segregated as in the 1960s. A newer discriminating lending practice was the subprime lending in the 1990s. Lenders targeted high-interest subprime loans to low-income and minority neighborhoods who might be eligible for fair-interest prime loans. Securitization, mortgage brokers and other non-deposit lenders, and legislative deregulation of the mortgage lending industry all played a role in promoting the subprime lending market.

https://en.wikipedia.org/wiki/Institutional_racism

"We Are the Voice of One" Prayer Declaration
(Declare Aloud)

We are the Voice of One that crieth in [city and state]: "Prepare Ye the way of the Lord!

Make straight in [city] a highway for our God; Every valley in [city] shall be exalted; And every mountain and hill in [city] shall be brought low. The crooked places in [city] shall be made straight; And the rough places shall be made smooth; And the glory of the Lord shall be revealed in [city and state]; And all of [city] and all nations shall see it together; for the mouth of the Lord has spoken it!"

Heavenly Father, we both claim and proclaim your prophecy that is written in Genesis 15: "Your descendants will be strangers in a foreign land; they will be slaves there and will be treated cruelly for **four hundred years**. But I will punish the nation that enslaves them, and when they leave that foreign land, they will take great wealth with them." Heavenly Father, make us one, just as You and the Lord Jesus are One! Heavenly Father, increase our numbers and gather Your people to pray! Let the Holy Spirit move freely, and the zeal of the Lord of Hosts shall accomplish it! In Jesus' name! Amen!

Offer a Closing Prayer to God
And as you pray....

- Consider the prayers of the enslaved as they lay on the slave ship, stored chained together and stored like cargo for months on an unknown journey that was thousands of miles long. The bodies of the enslaved who died in the Middle Passage were thrown in Atlantic Ocean.

- Imagine the prayers of the enslaved as they fled for freedom, following the North Star despite threats of lynching, beating, mutation, and death.

- Call out the names of the enslaved who were highlighted in today's reading from *The Underground Rail Road* and remember their descendants who still experience systemic racial oppression caused by social engineering.

Day 31

"Arthur came from Spring Hill, Maryland. Edward Fowler held Arthur in fetters and usurped authority over him as his lord and master. Arthur saw certain signs connected with his master's family which presaged to him that the day was not far distant, when somebody would have to be sold to raise money to pamper the appetites of some of the superior members of the patriarchal institution. Among these provocations were indulgence in a great deal of extravagance, and the growing up of a number of young masters and mistresses. Arthur would often look at the heirs, and the very thought of their coming into possession, would make him tremble. Nothing so affected Arthur's mind so much as moving him to make a bold stroke for freedom as these heirs. Under his old master, the usage had been bad enough, but he feared that it would be a great deal worse under the sons and daughters. He therefore wisely concluded to avoid the impending danger by availing himself of the Underground Rail Road. Arthur was about thirty years of age, medium size, and of a dark color.

The Underground Rail Road: A Record
(The True Story of Arthur Fowler, alias Benjamin Johnson, page 195)

· · · · · · ·

Institutional Racism

Institutional racism impacts health care accessibility within non-white minority communities by creating health disparities among racial groups. For example, from 1865 to 1906, many black veterans were unfairly denied disability pension by the union army disability pension system.

https://en.wikipedia.org/wiki/Institutional_racism

"We Are the Voice of One" Prayer Declaration
(Declare Aloud)

We are the Voice of One that crieth in [city and state]: "Prepare Ye the way of the Lord!

Make straight in [city] a highway for our God; Every valley in [city] shall be exalted; And every mountain and hill in [city] shall be brought low. The crooked places in [city] shall be made straight; And the rough places shall be made smooth; And the glory of the Lord shall be revealed in [city and state]; And all of [city] and all nations shall see it together; for the mouth of the Lord has spoken it!"

Heavenly Father, we both claim and proclaim your prophecy that is written in Genesis 15: "Your descendants will be strangers in a foreign land; they will be slaves there and will be treated cruelly for **four hundred years**. But I will punish the nation that enslaves them, and when they leave that foreign land, they will take great wealth with them." Heavenly Father, make us one, just as You and the Lord Jesus are One! Heavenly Father, increase our numbers and gather Your people to pray! Let the Holy Spirit move freely, and the zeal of the Lord of Hosts shall accomplish it! In Jesus' name! Amen!

Offer a Closing Prayer to God
And as you pray....

- Consider the prayers of the enslaved as they lay on the slave ship, stored chained together and stored like cargo for months on an unknown journey that was thousands of miles long. The bodies of the enslaved who died in the Middle Passage were thrown in Atlantic Ocean.

- Imagine the prayers of the enslaved as they fled for freedom, following the North Star despite threats of lynching, beating, mutation, and death.

- Call out the names of the enslaved who were highlighted in today's reading from The Underground Rail Road and remember their descendants who still experience systemic racial oppression caused by social engineering.

Day 32

"Harriet was a tall, well-made, intelligent young woman, twenty-two years of age. She spoke with feelings of much bitterness against her master, James Cuthbert, saying that he was a 'very hard man', at the same time adding that his 'wife was still worse'. Harriet 'had been sold once'....In escaping, she had to leave her 'poor old mother' with no hope of ever seeing her again; likewise, she regretted having to leave three brothers, who kindly aided her to escape. But having her heart bent on freedom, she resolved that nothing should deter her from putting forth efforts to get out of Slavery."

The Underground Rail Road: A Record
(The True Story of Harriet Mayor, Page 196)

· · · · · · · ·

Institutional Racism in Criminal Conviction

Although approximately two-thirds of crack cocaine users are white or Hispanic, a large percentage of people convicted of possession of crack cocaine in federal courts in 1994 were black....Racism at the institutional level dies hard, and is still prevalent in many U.S. institutions including law enforcement and the criminal justice system. Frequently these institutions use racial profiling along with greater police brutality. The greatest disparity is how capital punishment is disproportionately applied to minorities and especially to blacks. The gap is so wide it undermines any legitimacy of the death penalty along with the integrity of the whole judicial system.

https://en.wikipedia.org/wiki/Institutional_racism

"We are the Voice of One" Prayer Declaration
(Declare Aloud)

We are the Voice of One that crieth in [city and state]: "Prepare Ye the way of the Lord!

Make straight in [city] a highway for our God; Every valley in [city] shall be exalted; And every mountain and hill in [city] shall be brought low. The crooked places in [city] shall be made straight; And the rough places shall be made smooth; And the glory of the Lord shall be revealed in [city and state]; And all of [city] and all nations shall see it together; for the mouth of the Lord has spoken it!"

Heavenly Father, we both claim and proclaim your prophecy that is written in Genesis 15: "Your descendants will be strangers in a foreign land; they will be slaves there and will be treated cruelly for **four hundred years**. But I will punish the nation that enslaves them, and when they leave that foreign land, they will take great wealth with them." Heavenly Father, make us one, just as You and the Lord Jesus are One! Heavenly Father, increase our numbers and gather Your people to pray! Let the Holy Spirit move freely, and the zeal of the Lord of Hosts shall accomplish it! In Jesus' name! Amen!

Offer a Closing Prayer to God
And as you pray....

- Consider the prayers of the enslaved as they lay on the slave ship, stored chained together and stored like cargo for months on an unknown journey that was thousands of miles long. The bodies of the enslaved who died in the Middle Passage were thrown in Atlantic Ocean.

- Imagine the prayers of the enslaved as they fled for freedom, following the North Star despite threats of lynching, beating, mutation, and death.

- Call out the names of the enslaved who were highlighted in today's reading from The Underground Rail Road and remember their descendants who still experience systemic racial oppression caused by social engineering.

Day 33

"Daniel Bennett and his wife and children were the next in order. A woman poorly clad with a babe just one month old in her arms, and a little boy at her side, who could scarcely toddle, together with a husband who had never dared under penalty of the laws to protect her or her little ones, presented a most painfully touching picture. It was easy enough to see, that they had been crushed. The husband had been owned by Captain James Taylor — the wife and children by George Carter. The young mother gave Carter a very bad character, affirming, that it was a 'common practice with him to flog the slaves, stripped entirely naked' — that she had herself been so flogged, since she had been a married woman...He was about thirty-two — the wife about twenty-seven. Special pains were taken to provide aid and sympathy to this family in their destitution, fleeing under such peculiarly trying circumstances and from such loathsome brutality."

The Underground Rail Road: A Record
(The True Story of Daniel Bennett and His Wife, page 197)

· · · · · · ·

Shelby County v. Holder

This is a United States Supreme Court case ruling (2013) regarding the constitutionality of two provisions of the Voting Rights Act of 1965: (1) Section 5, which requires certain state and local governments to obtain federal preclearance before implementing any changes to their voting laws or practices; and (2) Section 4(b), which contains the coverage formula that determines which jurisdictions are subjected to preclearance based on their histories of discrimination in voting.

On June 25, 2013, the Court ruled by a 5-to-4 vote that Section 4(b) is unconstitutional because the coverage formula is based on data over forty years old, making it no longer responsive to current needs and therefore an impermissible burden on the constitutional principles of federalism and equal sovereignty of the states. The Court did not strike down Section 5, but without Section 4(b), no jurisdiction will be subject to Section 5 preclearance unless Congress enacts a new coverage formula.

Some critics have said that the ruling has made it easier for state officials to make it harder for black and other minority voters to vote. Five years after the ruling, nearly 1000 polling places had been closed in the U.S., with many of the closed polling places in predominantly African-American counties. Research shows that the changing of voter locations and reduction in voting locations can reduce voter turnout. There were also cuts to early voting, purges of voter rolls and imposition of strict voter ID laws.

https://en.wikipedia.org/wiki/Shelby_County_v._Holder

"We Are the Voice of One" Prayer Declaration
(Declare Aloud)

We are the Voice of One that crieth in [city and state]: "Prepare Ye the way of the Lord!

Make straight in [city] a highway for our God; Every valley in [city] shall be exalted; And every mountain and hill in [city] shall be brought low. The crooked places in [city] shall be made straight; And the rough places shall be made smooth; And the glory of the Lord shall be revealed in [city and state]; And all of [city] and all nations shall see it together; for the mouth of the Lord has spoken it!"

Heavenly Father, we both claim and proclaim your prophecy that is written in Genesis 15: "Your descendants will be strangers in a foreign land; they will be slaves there and will be treated cruelly for **four hundred years**. But I will punish the nation that enslaves them, and when they leave that foreign land, they will take great wealth with them." Heavenly Father, make us one, just as You and the Lord Jesus are One! Heavenly Father, increase our numbers and gather Your people to pray! Let the Holy Spirit move freely, and the zeal of the Lord of Hosts shall accomplish it! In Jesus' name! Amen!

Offer a Closing Prayer to God
And as you pray....

- Consider the prayers of the enslaved as they lay on the slave ship, stored chained together and stored like cargo for months on an unknown journey that was thousands of miles long. The bodies of the enslaved who died in the Middle Passage were thrown in Atlantic Ocean.

- Imagine the prayers of the enslaved as they fled for freedom, following the North Star despite threats of lynching, beating, mutation, and death.

- Call out the names of the enslaved who were highlighted in today's reading from *The Underground Rail Road* and remember their descendants who still experience systemic racial oppression caused by social engineering.

Day 34 _____

"Sarah, having no one to care for her, and, having been threatened with the auction-block, mustered pluck and started out in search of a new home among strangers beyond the borders of slave territory. According to her story, she 'was born free' in the State of Delaware but had been 'bound out' to a man by the name of George Churchman, living in Wilmington. Here she averred, that she 'had been flogged repeatedly', and had been other wise ill-treated, while no one interfered to take her part. Consequently, she concluded, that although she was born free, she would not like to be benefited thereby unless she made her escape on the Underground Rail Road. This idea of freedom continued to agitate Sarah's mind until she decided to leave forthwith. She was a young mulatto woman, single, and told her story of hardships and of the dread of being sold, in a manner to elicit much sympathy. She had a mother living in New Castle, named Ann Eliza Kingslow. It was no uncommon thing for free-born persons in slave States to lose their birth-right in a manner similar to that by which Sarah feared that she had lost hers."

The Underground Rail Road: A Record
(The True Story of Sarah A. Dunagan, page 200)

• • • • • • •

Background of *Shelby County v. Holder*

Congress enacted the Voting Rights Act of 1965 to address entrenched racial discrimination in voting, "an insidious and pervasive evil which had been perpetuated in certain parts of our country through unremitting and ingenious defiance of the Constitution." Section 5 of the Act contains a "preclearance" requirement that requires certain states and local governments to obtain a determination by the United States Attorney General or a three-judge panel of the United States District Court for the District of Columbia that changes to their voting laws or practices do not "deny or abridge the right to vote on account of race, color, or membership in a language minority group", before those changes may be enforced. Section 4(b) contains the coverage formula that determines which states and local governments are subject to preclearance under Section 5. The formula covers jurisdictions that, as of November 1964, November 1968, or November 1972, maintained a prohibited "test or device" as a condition of registering to vote or voting and had a voting-age population of which less than 50 percent either were registered to vote or actually voted in that year's presidential election. Section 4(a) allows covered jurisdictions that have made sufficient progress in ending discriminatory voting practices to "bail out" of the preclearance requirement.

https://en.wikipedia.org/wiki/Shelby_County_v._Holder

"We Are the Voice of One" Prayer Declaration
(Declare Aloud)

We are the Voice of One that crieth in [city and state]: "Prepare Ye the way of the Lord!

Make straight in [city] a highway for our God; Every valley in [city] shall be exalted; And every mountain and hill in [city] shall be brought low. The crooked places in [city] shall be made straight; And the rough places shall be made smooth; And the glory of the Lord shall be revealed in [city and state]; And all of [city] and all nations shall see it together; for the mouth of the Lord has spoken it!"

Heavenly Father, we both claim and proclaim your prophecy that is written in Genesis 15: "Your descendants will be strangers in a foreign land; they will be slaves there and will be treated cruelly for **four hundred years**. But I will punish the nation that enslaves them, and when they leave that foreign land, they will take great wealth with them." Heavenly Father, make us one, just as You and the Lord Jesus are One! Heavenly Father, increase our numbers and gather Your people to pray! Let the Holy Spirit move freely, and the zeal of the Lord of Hosts shall accomplish it! In Jesus' name! Amen!

Offer a Closing Prayer to God
And as you pray....

- Consider the prayers of the enslaved as they lay on the slave ship, stored chained together and stored like cargo for months on an unknown journey that was thousands of miles long. The bodies of the enslaved who died in the Middle Passage were thrown in Atlantic Ocean.

- Imagine the prayers of the enslaved as they fled for freedom, following the North Star despite threats of lynching, beating, mutation, and death.

- Call out the names of the enslaved who were highlighted in today's reading from *The Underground Rail Road* and remember their descendants who still experience systemic racial oppression caused by social engineering.

Day 35

"James was twenty-seven years of age…The heel of a woman, by the name of Mrs. Ann McCourt, had been on James' neck, and she had caused him to suffer severely. …He plainly stated that she was a 'desperate woman' — that he had 'never known any good of her,' and that he was moved to escape to get rid of her. In other words she had threatened to sell him; this well nigh produced frenzy in James' mind, for too well did he remember, that he had already been sold three times, and in different stages of his bondage had been treated quite cruelly. In the change of masters he was positive in saying, that he had not found a good one, and, besides, he entertained the belief that such personages were very rare."

The Underground Rail Road: A Record
(The True Story of James Morris, page 202)

· · · · · · ·

The Southern Strategy

As a member of the Reagan administration in 1981, Lee Atwater gave an anonymous interview to political scientist Alexander P. Lamis. Part of the interview was printed in Lamis' book *The Two-Party South*, then reprinted in *Southern Politics* in the 1990s with Atwater's name revealed.

Atwater: As to the whole Southern strategy that Harry S. Dent, Sr. and others put together in 1968, opposition to the Voting Rights Act would have been a central part of keeping the South. Now you don't have to do that. All that you need to do to keep the South is for Reagan to run in place on the issues that he's campaigned on since 1964, and that's fiscal conservatism, balancing the budget, cut taxes, you know, the whole cluster.

Questioner: But the fact is, isn't it, that Reagan does get to the Wallace voter and to the racist side of the Wallace voter by doing away with legal services, by cutting down on Food Stamps?

Atwater: Y'all don't quote me on this. You start out in 1954 by saying, "Nigger, nigger, nigger." By 1968 you can't say "nigger"—

that hurts you. Backfires. So you say stuff like forced busing, states' rights and all that stuff. You're getting so abstract now [that] you're talking about cutting taxes, and all these things you're talking about are totally economic things and a byproduct of them is [that] blacks get hurt worse than whites. And subconsciously maybe that is part of it. I'm not saying that. But I'm saying that if it is getting that abstract, and that coded, that we are doing away with the racial problem one way or the other. You follow me—because obviously sitting around saying, "We want to cut this", is much more abstract than even the busing thing, and a hell of a lot more abstract than "Nigger, nigger." So, any way you look at it, race is coming on the backbone.

https://en.wikipedia.org/wiki/Lee_Atwater

"We Are the Voice of One" Prayer Declaration
(Declare Aloud)

We are the Voice of One that crieth in [city and state]: "Prepare Ye the way of the Lord!

Make straight in [city] a highway for our God; Every valley in [city] shall be exalted; And every mountain and hill in [city] shall be brought low. The crooked places in [city] shall be made straight; And the rough places shall be made smooth; And the glory of the Lord shall be revealed in [city and state]; And all of [city] and all nations shall see it together; for the mouth of the Lord has spoken it!"

Heavenly Father, we both claim and proclaim your prophecy that is written in Genesis 15: "Your descendants will be strangers in a foreign land; they will be slaves there and will be treated cruelly for **four hundred years**. But I will punish the nation that enslaves them, and when they leave that foreign land, they will take great wealth with them." Heavenly Father, make us one, just as You and the Lord Jesus are One! Heavenly Father, increase our numbers and gather Your people to pray! Let the Holy Spirit move freely, and the zeal of the Lord of Hosts shall accomplish it! In Jesus' name! Amen!

Offer a Closing Prayer to God
And as you pray....

- Consider the prayers of the enslaved as they lay on the slave ship, stored chained together and stored like cargo for months on an unknown journey that was thousands of miles long. The bodies of the enslaved who died in the Middle Passage were thrown in Atlantic Ocean.

- Imagine the prayers of the enslaved as they fled for freedom, following the North Star despite threats of lynching, beating, mutation, and death.

- Call out the names of the enslaved who were highlighted in today's reading from *The Underground Rail Road* and remember their descendants who still experience systemic racial oppression caused by social engineering.

Day 36

"Nancy was also from Richmond...She was neat, modest, and well-behaved — with a good figure and the picture of health, with a countenance beaming with joy and gladness, notwithstanding the late struggles and sufferings through which she had passed. Young as she was, she had seen much of slavery, and had doubtless, profited by the lessons thereof. At all events, it was through cruel treatment, having been frequently beaten after she had passed her eighteenth year, that she was prompted to seek freedom. It was so common for her mistress to give way to unbridled passions that Nancy never felt safe. Under the severest infliction of punishment, she was not allowed to complain. Neither from mistress nor master had she any reason to expect mercy or leniency...It was true that the master, Mr. William Bears, was a Yankee from Connecticut, and his wife a member of the Episcopal Church, but Nancy's yoke seemed none the lighter for all that."

The Underground Rail Road: A Record
(The True Story of Nancy Brister, page 237)

. . . .

Discrimination by the United States Department of Agriculture

From 1981 to 1997, the United States Department of Agriculture discriminated against tens of thousands of black American farmers, denying loans that were provided to white farmers in similar circumstances.

https://en.wikipedia.org/wiki/Racism_in_the_United_States

"We Are the Voice of One" Prayer Declaration
(Declare Aloud)

We are the Voice of One that crieth in [city and state]: "Prepare Ye the way of the Lord!

Make straight in [city] a highway for our God; Every valley in [city] shall be exalted; And every mountain and hill in [city] shall be brought low. The crooked places in [city] shall be made straight; And the rough places shall be made smooth; And the glory of the Lord shall be revealed in [city and state]; And all of [city] and all nations shall see it together; for the mouth of the Lord has spoken it!"

Heavenly Father, we both claim and proclaim your prophecy that is written in Genesis 15: "Your descendants will be strangers in a foreign land; they will be slaves there and will be treated cruelly for **four hundred years**. But I will punish the nation that enslaves them, and when they leave that foreign land, they will take great wealth with them." Heavenly Father, make us one, just as You and the Lord Jesus are One! Heavenly Father, increase our numbers and gather Your people to pray! Let the Holy Spirit move freely, and the zeal of the Lord of Hosts shall accomplish it! In Jesus' name! Amen!

Offer a Closing Prayer to God
And as you pray....

- Consider the prayers of the enslaved as they lay on the slave ship, stored chained together and stored like cargo for months on an

unknown journey that was thousands of miles long. The bodies of the enslaved who died in the Middle Passage were thrown in Atlantic Ocean.

- Imagine the prayers of the enslaved as they fled for freedom, following the North Star despite threats of lynching, beating, mutation, and death.

- Call out the names of the enslaved who were highlighted in today's reading from *The Underground Rail Road* and remember their descendants who still experience systemic racial oppression caused by social engineering.

Day 37

"Andrew...was twenty-six years of age, and a decidedly inviting-looking specimen of the peculiar institution...He, with his wife and one child, belong to a small orphan girl, who lived at South End, Camden County, N.C. His wife and child had to be left behind. While it seemed very hard for a husband thus to leave his wife, every one that did so weakened slavery and encouraged and strengthened anti-slavery."

The Underground Rail Road: A Record
(The True Story of Andrew Shepherd, page 239)

· · · · · · ·

American Descendants of Slavery (#ADOS)

#ADOS was started by the brain trust of Howard graduate and host of the Breaking Brown political show, Yvette Carnell, and UCLA alumnus and attorney, Antonio Moore who hosts the weekly radio show Tonetalks. ADOS—which stands for American Descendants of Slavery—seeks to reclaim/restore the critical national character of the African American identity and experience, one grounded in our group's unique lineage, and which is central to our continuing struggle for social and economic justice in the United States. – Antonio Moore

http://ados101.com/about-ados

"We Are the Voice of One" Prayer Declaration
(Declare Aloud)

We are the Voice of One that crieth in [city and state]: "Prepare Ye the way of the Lord!

Make straight in [city] a highway for our God; Every valley in [city] shall be exalted; And every mountain and hill in [city] shall be brought low. The crooked places in [city] shall be made straight; And the rough places shall be made smooth; And the glory of the Lord shall be revealed in [city and state]; And all of [city] and all nations shall see it together; for the mouth of the Lord has spoken it!"

Heavenly Father, we both claim and proclaim your prophecy that is written in Genesis 15: "Your descendants will be strangers in a foreign land; they will be slaves there and will be treated cruelly for **four hundred years**. But I will punish the nation that enslaves them, and when they leave that foreign land, they will take great wealth with them." Heavenly Father, make us one, just as You and the Lord Jesus are One! Heavenly Father, increase our numbers and gather Your people to pray! Let the Holy Spirit move freely, and the zeal of the Lord of Hosts shall accomplish it! In Jesus' name! Amen!

Offer a Closing Prayer to God
And as you pray....

- Consider the prayers of the enslaved as they lay on the slave ship, stored chained together and stored like cargo for months on an unknown journey that was thousands of miles long. The bodies of the enslaved who died in the Middle Passage were thrown in Atlantic Ocean.

- Imagine the prayers of the enslaved as they fled for freedom, following the North Star despite threats of lynching, beating, mutation, and death.

- Call out the names of the enslaved who were highlighted in today's reading from *The Underground Rail Road* and remember their descendants who still experience systemic racial oppression caused by social engineering.

Day 38

"Winnie Patty, and her daughter, Elizabeth, arrived safely from Norfolk, Va. The mother is about twenty-two years of age, good looking and of chestnut color, smart and brave. From the latter part of October 1855, to the latter part of March, 1856, this young slave mother, with her child, was secreted under the floor of a house. The house was occupied by a slave family, friends of Winnie. During the cold winter weather, she suffered severely from wet and cold, getting considerably frosted, but her faith failed not, even in the hour of greatest extremity. She chose rather to suffer thus than endure slavery any longer, especially as she was aware that the auction-block awaited her. She had already been sold three times; she knew therefore what it was to be sold. Jacob Shuster was the name of the man whom she spoke of as her tormentor and master, and from whom she fled."

The Underground Rail Road: A Record
(The True Story of Winnie Patty and her daughter, page 243)

· · · · · · ·

The Creation of an #ADOS Underclass
Served as the Financial Engine of a Nation

In his book, **American Slavery, American Freedom**, historian Edmund Morgan concludes that slavery was not a contradiction of American freedom, but rather that slavery was the institution that made white freedom possible. In other words, slavery was not a mistake so much as a precondition for a societal hierarchy which requires descendants of slaves to remain a bottom caste and be made to suffer the necessary failures of a brutal economic system. This was followed by a Jim Crow-era that saw #ADOS become actual contagions that lead to a destruction of wealth; through federally-supported, discriminatory practices like redlining, black presence literally made wealth disappear in communities, all while American whites—and more recently, immigrants— enjoy advantage in a land of apparently equal opportunity that was in fact manufactured on the back of black failure.

According to Yale historian David Blight, "by 1860, there were more millionaires (slaveholders all) living in the lower Mississippi Valley than anywhere else in the United States. In the same year, the nearly four million American slaves were worth some $3.5 billion, making them the largest single financial asset in the entire U.S. economy, worth more than all manufacturing and railroads combined."

Codified by government and exploited by private actors, the creation of an #ADOS underclass served as the financial engine of a nation that never recognized the debt it owed to the group as a result. As such, the #ADOS movement is underpinned by the demand for reparative justice in making the group whole, and as a necessary component in fulfilling the promise of opportunity from which, by design, ADOS have been historically excluded and denied.

– Antonio Moore

http://ados101.com/about-ados

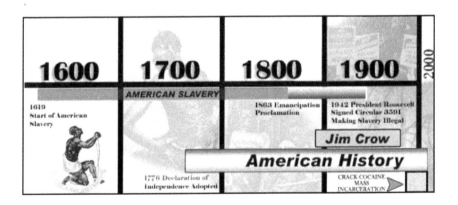

We Are the Voice of One" Prayer Declaration
(Declare Aloud)

We are the Voice of One that crieth in [city and state]: "Prepare Ye the way of the Lord!

Make straight in [city] a highway for our God; Every valley in [city] shall be exalted; And every mountain and hill in [city] shall be brought low. The crooked places in [city] shall be made straight; And the rough places shall be made smooth; And the glory of the Lord shall be revealed in [city and state]; And all of [city] and all nations shall see it together; for the mouth of the Lord has spoken it!"

Heavenly Father, we both claim and proclaim your prophecy that is written in Genesis 15: "Your descendants will be strangers in a foreign land; they will be slaves there and will be treated cruelly for **four hundred years**. But I will punish the nation that enslaves them, and when they leave that foreign land, they will take great wealth with them." Heavenly Father, make us one, just as You and the Lord Jesus are One! Heavenly Father, increase our numbers and gather Your people to pray! Let the Holy Spirit move freely, and the zeal of the Lord of Hosts shall accomplish it! In Jesus' name! Amen!

Offer a Closing Prayer to God
And as you pray....

- Consider the prayers of the enslaved as they lay on the slave ship, stored chained together and stored like cargo for months on an unknown journey that was thousands of miles long. The bodies of the enslaved who died in the Middle Passage were thrown in Atlantic Ocean.

- Imagine the prayers of the enslaved as they fled for freedom, following the North Star despite threats of lynching, beating, mutation, and death.

- Call out the names of the enslaved who were highlighted in today's reading from *The Underground Rail Road* and remember their descendants who still experience systemic racial oppression caused by social engineering.

Day 39

"He was about forty-six years of age, according to his reckoning, full six feet high, and in muscular appearance was very rugged, and in his countenance were evident marks of firmness. He said that he was born a slave in North Carolina and had been sold three times. He was first sold when he was a child three years of age, the second time when he was thirteen years old, and the third and last time from Jesse Moore, from whom he fled...'In the woods I lived on nothing, you may say, and something too. I had bread, and roasting ears, and 'taters. I stayed in the hollow of a big poplar tree for seven months; the other part of the time I stayed in a cave. I suffered mighty bad with the cold and for something to eat...while in the woods all my thoughts was how to get away to a free country."

The Underground Rail Road: A Record
(The True Story of Harry Grimes, page 269)

· · · · · · ·

The ADOS Truth

The truth of ADOS life is seen nowhere more clearly than the racial wealth gap in this country" – Antonio Moore

http://ados101.com/about-ados

"We Are the Voice of One" Prayer Declaration
(Declare Aloud)

We are the Voice of One that crieth in [city and state]: "Prepare Ye the way of the Lord!

Make straight in [city] a highway for our God; Every valley in [city] shall be exalted; And every mountain and hill in [city] shall be brought low. The crooked places in [city] shall be made straight; And the rough places shall be made smooth; And the glory of the Lord shall be revealed in [city and state]; And all of [city] and all nations shall see it together; for the mouth of the Lord has spoken it!"

Heavenly Father, we both claim and proclaim your prophecy that is written in Genesis 15: "Your descendants will be strangers in a foreign land; they will be slaves there and will be treated cruelly for **four hundred years**. But I will punish the nation that enslaves them, and when they leave that foreign land, they will take great wealth with them." Heavenly Father, make us one, just as You and the Lord Jesus are One! Heavenly Father, increase our numbers and gather Your people to pray! Let the Holy Spirit move freely, and the zeal of the Lord of Hosts shall accomplish it! In Jesus' name! Amen!

Offer a Closing Prayer to God
And as you pray....

- Consider the prayers of the enslaved as they lay on the slave ship, stored chained together and stored like cargo for months on an unknown journey that was thousands of miles long. The bodies of the enslaved who died in the Middle Passage were thrown in Atlantic Ocean.

- Imagine the prayers of the enslaved as they fled for freedom, following the North Star despite threats of lynching, beating, mutation, and death.

- Call out the names of the enslaved who were highlighted in today's reading from *The Underground Rail Road* and remember their descendants who still experience systemic racial oppression caused by social engineering.

Day 40

"Abram was thirty-five years of age, chestnut color, common size, with a scar over the left eye, and another on the upper lip. 'I was held as the property of the late Taylor Sewell, but when I escaped I was in the service of W.C. Williams, a commission merchant....I felt if I stayed and got old no one would care for me, I wouldn't be of no account to nobody.' 'But are not the old slaves well cared for by their masters?" a member of the Committee here remarked. "Take care of them! No!" Abram replied with much earnestness, and then went on to explain how such property was left to perish. Said Abram. "There was an old man named Ike, who belonged to the same estate that I did, he was treated like a dog; after they could get no more work out of him, they said, 'let him die, he is of no service; there is no use of getting a doctor for him.' Accordingly, there could be no other fate for the old man but to suffer and died with creepers in his legs.' It was sickening to hear him narrate instances of similar suffering in the case of old slaves. Abram left two sisters and one brother in bondage."

The Underground Rail Road: A Record
(The True Story of Abram Wooders, page 261)

• • • • • • •

A Consequence of Lack of Wealth Transfers and Multi-generational Oppression

Duke University economist Dr. William "Sandy" Darity, and co-founder of the ADOS movement, Antonio Moore, along with other researchers, observed in their study "What We Get Wrong About Closing the Racial Wealth Gap," that the concentration of ADOS at the bottom economically is a consequence of lack of wealth transfers and multi-generational oppression, not individual agency or cultural patterns. – Antonio Moore

http://ados101.com/about-ados

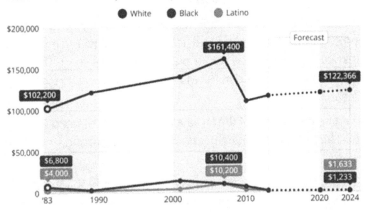

Racial Wealth Inequality Is Rampant In The U.S.
Median household wealth by race/ethnicity in the United States (1983–2024)

● White ● Black ● Latino

Forecast

$200,000
$161,400
$150,000
$122,366
$102,200
$100,000
$50,000
$6,800
$10,400
$1,633
$4,000
$10,200
$1,233
0

'83   1990   2000   2010   2020   2024

@StatistaCharts Source: Prosperity Now & Institute For Policy Studies

Forbes statista

"We Are the Voice of One" Prayer Declaration
(Declare Aloud)

We are the Voice of One that crieth in [city and state]: "Prepare Ye the way of the Lord!

Make straight in [city] a highway for our God; Every valley in [city] shall be exalted; And every mountain and hill in [city] shall be brought low. The crooked places in [city] shall be made straight; And the rough places shall be made smooth; And the glory of the Lord shall be revealed in [city and state]; And all of [city] and all nations shall see it together; for the mouth of the Lord has spoken it!"

Heavenly Father, we both claim and proclaim your prophecy that is written in Genesis 15: "Your descendants will be strangers in a foreign land; they will be slaves there and will be treated cruelly for **four hundred years**. But I will punish the nation that enslaves them, and when they leave that foreign land, they will take great wealth with them." Heavenly Father, make us one, just as You and the Lord Jesus are One! Heavenly Father, increase our numbers and gather Your people to pray! Let the Holy Spirit move freely, and the zeal of the Lord of Hosts shall accomplish it! In Jesus' name! Amen!

Offer a Closing Prayer to God
And as you pray....

- Consider the prayers of the enslaved as they lay on the slave ship, stored chained together and stored like cargo for months on an unknown journey that was thousands of miles long. The bodies of the enslaved who died in the Middle Passage were thrown in Atlantic Ocean.

- Imagine the prayers of the enslaved as they fled for freedom, following the North Star despite threats of lynching, beating, mutation, and death.

- Call out the names of the enslaved who were highlighted in today's reading from The Underground Rail Road and remember their descendants who still experience systemic racial oppression caused by social engineering.

Bibliography & Recommended Reading

Anderson, PhD, Carol, *White Rage: The Unspoken Truth of Our Racial Divide*. New York: Bloomsbury USA, 2016

Alexander, Michelle, *The New Jim Crow: Mass Incarceration in the Age of Colorblindness*. New York: The New Press, 2012

Baptist, Edward E. *The Half Has Never Been Told: Slavery and the Making of American Capitalism*. New York: Basic Books, 2014

Baradaran, Mehrsa, *The Color of Money: Black Banks and the Racial Wealth Gap*. Cambridge, Mass.: Belknap Press, 2017

Rothstein, Richard, *The Color of Law: A Forgotten History of How Our Government Segregated America*. New York: Liveright, 2017.

Still, William, *The Underground Rail Road: A Record*. Philadelphia: Porter & Coates, 1872.

Suggested Uses

Churches and organizations can use *40 Days of Prayer* during the first 40 days of the year in observance of the signing of the Emancipation Proclamation on January 1, 1863.

Groups can engage in *40 Days of Prayer* during the Lenten season, in the forty days leading to Easter.

Churches or groups can commit to in *40 Days of Prayer* in celebration of a major event in the life of the organization (anniversary, special day celebration, etc.)

Local African-American and white congregations can establish partnerships and complete *40 Days of Prayer* together and then conclude with a worship service and fellowship meal.

Local African-American and white religious entities (i.e. Baptist Associations, Presbyteries, Districts, etc.) can establish partnerships and complete *40 Days of Prayer* together and then conclude with a worship service and fellowship meal.

About Cheri L. Mills

For twenty-five years, Cheri L. Mills has served in full-time ministry at St. Stephen Baptist Church in Louisville, Kentucky under the leadership of Rev. Dr. Kevin W. Cosby, senior pastor. Cheri serves as church administrator at St. Stephen and administrative assistant to the senior pastor. She teaches adult Sunday School there and serves in the church's prayer ministry.

Cheri is also prayer director for the Prayer Department at Simmons College of Kentucky, the nation's 107th HBCU (Historically Black Colleges and Universities), where Dr. Cosby serves as president.

She holds a bachelor's degree from Western Kentucky University and is a candidate for a Master of Divinity degree from the Baptist Seminary of Kentucky.

Cheri is the visionary leader and founder of 1 Voice Prayer Movement, which unites churches across racial, denominational, and cultural lines to pray on behalf of their cities, states, nation, and world that God's justice will be dispensed on behalf of the poor and oppressed. As of November 2019, 1 Voice Prayer Movement celebrates ten years of intercessory prayer ministry.

She was awarded the Mary McLeod Bethune Achievement Award by the Louisville Section of the National Council of Negro Women, Inc. for her contributions impacting the community, city, state, and beyond.

H.R.40

Commission to Study and Develop Reparation Proposals for African-Americans Act

To address the fundamental injustice, cruelty, brutality, and inhumanity of slavery in the United States and the 13 American colonies between 1619 and 1865 and to establish a commission to study and consider a national apology and proposal for reparations for the institution of slavery, its subsequent de jure and de facto racial and economic discrimination against African-Americans, and the impact of these forces on living African-Americans, to make recommendations to the Congress on appropriate remedies, and for other purposes.

For more information about H.R.40, visit www.congress.gov.

Take Action!

Contact your congressional representative to support H.R.40.